A R
Road

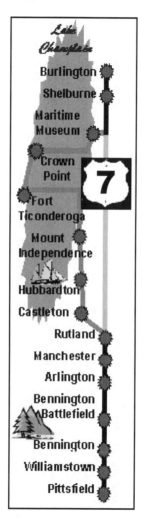

Spend a Revolutionary Day Along
One of America's Most Historic Routes

OTHER REVOLUTIONARY WAR ROAD TRIPS
By Raymond C. Houghton

A Revolutionary War Road Trip on US Route 4
(Castleton, VT to Albany, NY)

A Revolutionary War Road Trip on US Route 9W
(New York City to Kingston, NY)

A Revolutionary War Road *Trip* on US Route 9
(Kings Ferry, NY to Saratoga Springs, NY)

A Revolutionary War Road Trip on US Route 202
(Elks Neck, MD to Philadelphia, PA)

A Revolutionary War Boat Trip on the Champlain Canal
(Bethlehem, NY to Champlain Maritime Museum, VT)

A Revolutionary War Road Trip on US Route 20
(Albany, NY to Boston, MA, in preparation)

A Revolutionary War Road Trip on US Route 60
(Charlottesville, VA to Yorktown, VA, in preparation)

A Revolutionary War Road Trip on the Mohawk Turnpike
(Oswego, NY to Schenectady, NY, in preparation)

A Revolutionary War Road Trip on US Route 221
(Chesnee, SC to Augusta, GA, in preparation)

A Revolutionary War Road Trip on US Route 7

Spend a Revolutionary Day Along
One of America's Most Historic Routes

Raymond C. Houghton

Cyber Haus
Delmar, NY

A Revolutionary War Road Trip on US Route 7
Spend a Revolutionary Day Along
One of America's Most Historic Routes

Copyright © 2004 by Cyber Haus.
All rights reserved.

Revolutionary War Road Trips
are published by Cyber Haus
and printed on-demand
by Booksurge, LLC,
www.booksurge.com,
1-866-308-6235.

ISBN: 1-931373-10-8

Cyber Haus
159 Delaware Avenue, #145
Delmar, NY 12054
www.revolutionaryday.com
www.cyhaus.com
cyhaus@msn.com
518-478-9798

In memory of
Daniel Houghton
and William French,
who gave their lives for
Vermont independence at the
Westminster Massacre,
March 13, 1775

INTRODUCTION

US Route 7 goes from the Long Island Sound to the Canadian Border passing through western parts of Connecticut, Massachusetts and Vermont. There are many historic areas to discover and explore along this route, especially between Pittsfield, Massachusetts and Burlington, Vermont -- history that dates back to three very important years in the United States' struggle for independence: 1775, 1776 and 1777. This book presents a one-day, road trip through these areas, but be warned, with so much to see, it could easily take a week.

British General Burgoyne once described the people of this area as "the most rebellious race on the continent and hangs like a gathering storm upon my left." Burgoyne, who was leading the 1777 British invasion from Canada to split the colonies along the Champlain and Hudson valleys, was no doubt frustrated by the stubbornness of its citizens who would not surrender to his invading army. Actually, this area covers some of the most beautiful country in the northeast. It's no wonder that its citizens would defend it with their lives.

A Revolutionary War Road Trip on US Route 7 begins early in the morning in Pittsfield, Massachusetts, historically on May 1, 1775 where

Edward Mott and a squad of Connecticut volunteers met with John Brown to recruit volunteers and discuss an assault on Fort Ticonderoga. From Pittsfield, you will go north along US Route 7 through Williamstown, Massachusetts to Bennington, Vermont where on May 3, 1775, a platoon of Massachusetts and Connecticut volunteers met with Ethan Allen and the Green Mountain Boys.

From Bennington, you will detour slightly to the west to visit the Bennington Battlefield in Hoosick Falls, New York then return back to Vermont and travel north along Historic Route 7A (old US Route 7) through Arlington to Manchester. From Manchester, you will continue north on US Route 7 to Rutland then detour west along Historic Route 4A to Castleton where on May 9, 1775, a battalion-sized force from Vermont, Massachusetts and Connecticut would make final plans for an assault on Fort Ticonderoga.

From Castleton you will head north on the old military road making visits to the Hubbardton Battlefield and Mount Independence, then cross Lake Champlain by ferry to Fort Ticonderoga, New York where early in the morning on May 10, 1775, British Captain Delaplace would surrender the fort to Ethan Allen after a surprise attack by American forces.

From Fort Ticonderoga, you will resume a northerly direction on the west side of Lake Champlain up to Crown Point. After crossing the bridge over Lake Champlain, you will travel up the east side of the lake to the Lake Champlain Maritime Museum, then work your way back to US Route 7 and finish your tour in Burlington, Vermont where in 1787, Ethan Allen and his wife, Fannie, would settle into their final home.

So, if you're ready begin **A Revolutionary Day** along historic US Route 7.

TABLE OF CONTENTS AND TRIP LOG

Early Morning -- *Mile Mark 0.0* ....Page 17

Pittsfield, Massachusetts: On May 1st, 1775 at Easton's Tavern, John Brown and James Easton of Pittsfield and Edward Mott of Connecticut met here to begin planning the first offensive military action against the British in the Revolutionary War -- the capture of Fort Ticonderoga.

Mile Mark 0.0 - 20.6 ....Page 23

Pittsfield to Williamstown: Travel up US Route 7, alongside Pontoosuc Lake and Mount Greylock, the tallest mountain in Massachusetts.

Mile Mark 20.6 - 22.5...................................Page 26

Williamstown, Massachusetts: Pass through the home of Williams College, which also was a recruiting stop in 1775.

Mile Mark 22.5 - 34.9...................................Page 30

Williamstown to Old Bennington: Cross the Vermont-Massachusetts border and travel into the Green Mountain State, home of the Green Mountain Boys.

Mid-Morning -- Mile *Mark 34.9 - 35.4*..............Page 33

Old Bennington, Vermont: On May 3rd, 1775 at the Catamount Inn, Ethan Allen met with Edward Mott, John Brown and James Easton to discuss the capture of Fort Ticonderoga. Two years later, Bennington's storehouses would be an unsuccessful target of Burgoyne's British invasion from Canada.

Mile Mark 35.4 - 44.9 .... Page 45

Old Bennington to the Bennington Battlefield: Detour across the Vermont-New York border to the battlefield area where Americans chose to intercept the invading British Forces.

Mile Mark 44.9 - 47.2.................................. Page 53

Bennington Battlefield, New York: Visit the hilltop where British forces under the command of Lieutenant Colonel Friedrick Baum, were surrounded and engaged by American Forces from New Hampshire, Massachusetts and Vermont. The British Forces surrendered on August 16, 1777.

Mile Mark 47.2 - 63.8.................................. Page 59

Bennington Battlefield to Arlington: Return back to Vermont and turn north onto historic Route 7A (old US Route 7). Follow Route 7A into Arlington.

Late Morning -- *Mile Mark 63.8 - 64.0* .... Page 60

Arlington, Vermont: In 1775, patriot forces led by Ethan Allen passed through Arlington on their way to Fort Ticonderoga.

Mile Mark 64.0 - 72.1 .... Page 63

Arlington to Manchester: Follow Route 7A past the Ira Allen house and into Manchester.

Mile Mark 72.1.. Page 65

Manchester, Vermont: In 1775, Manchester was a crossroad to Fort Ticonderoga, but also a crossroad to a much larger American army, this one in retreat in 1777.

Mile Mark 72.1 - 104.9.................................Page 68

Manchester to Rutland: Rejoin US Route 7 and travel north to Rutland.

Mile Mark 104.9..Page 72

Rutland, Vermont: Briefly visit two memorials placed by the Daughters of the American Revolution.

Mile Mark 104.9 - 116.0..............................Page 76

Rutland to Castleton: After a break for lunch, begin another detour to the west, this one along Route 4A to Castleton.

Early Afternoon -- *Mile Mark 116.0 - 117.2*.....Page 76

Castleton, Vermont: In the spring of 1775, Ethan Allen, Seth Warner, Edward Mott, John Brown and Benedict Arnold met here to make final plans for the attack on Fort Ticonderoga and Fort Crown Point.

Mile Mark 117.2 - 123.8..............................Page 79

Castleton to the Hubbardton Battlefield: Travel up the old military road to the Hubbardton Battlefield.

Mile Mark 123.8..Page 80

Hubbardton Battlefield, Vermont: On July 7, 1777, British forces attacked the rear guard of the American forces that were retreating down the military road from Fort Ticonderoga.

Mile Mark 123.8 - 146.3 .... Page 89

Hubbardton Battlefield to Mount Independence: Continue your travels up the old military road to Mount Independence.

Mid Afternoon -- Mile *Mark 146.3* .... Page 94

Mount Independence, Vermont: Visit the winter home for about 2,000 American troops from 1776-1777.

Mile 146.3 - 158.8 .... Page 99

Mount Independence to Fort Ticonderoga: Travel up the east side of Lake Champlain and take the Ticonderoga Ferry to New York State.

Mile Mark 158.8 .... Page 105

Fort Ticonderoga, New York: Visit the restored Fort Ticonderoga. No fort in the world has had such an active, yet short history. In two decades, this fort was targeted by great nations six times, four of these between 1775 and 1777.

Late Afternoon -- *Mile Mark 158.8 - 176.5* .... Page 114

Fort Ticonderoga to Fort Crown Point: Continue traveling up the old military road.

Mile Mark 176.5 - 177.1 .... Page 119

Fort Crown Point, New York: Visit the impressive ruins of Fort Crown Point, which includes redoubts, barracks and parade ground.

Mile Mark 177.1 - 191.1 .... Page 127

Fort Crown Point to the Maritime Museum: Return back to Vermont and travel up the east side of Lake Champlain.

Mile Mark 191.1..Page 130

Lake Champlain Maritime Museum, Vermont: Tour a full-sized, 54-foot replica of Benedict Arnold's 1776 gunboat, the Philadelphia II.

Early Evening -- *Mile Mark 191.1 - 211.2* ....Page 132

Maritime Museum to Shelburne: Return back to US Route 7 at Vergennes.

Mile Mark 211.2 - 211.4.............................Page 134

Shelburne: Home of the expansive Shelburne Museum.

Mile Mark 211.4 - 221.5.............................Page 136

Shelburne to Burlington: Drive to the historical conclusion of your **Revolutionary Day** in Burlington.

Mile Mark 221.5...Page 138

Burlington, Vermont: Visit the Ethan Allen Homestead.

Bibliography ....Page 149

About the Author ....Page 151

> **Ethan Allen's Route to Ticonderoga**
>
> 1 May 1775 — Edward Mott and the Connecticut Volunteers march to Pittsfield, Massachusetts, where they join John Brown and James Easton.
>
> (Fort Ticonderoga Exhibit)

PITTSFIELD

"One thing I must mention to be kept as profound secret — the fort at Ticonderoga must be seized as soon as possible should hostilities be committed by the King's Troops. The people of New Hampshire Grants [Vermont] have engaged to do this business and in my opinion, they are the most proper persons for the job," — American Agent John Brown, March 29, 1775.

On May 1, 1775, John Brown, Captain Edward Mott and Colonel James Easton met here at Easton's tavern to make initial plans to seize badly needed artillery and munitions from the British at Fort Ticonderoga for the defense of Boston. This was the first time Americans were considering an offensive military action against the British. Prior to this time, Americans had either defended against offensive actions, such as Lexington and Concord, or responded by organizing demonstrations, such as the Boston Tea Party.

At the time of the meeting at Easton's Tavern, the patriot forces consisted of:

- Edward Mott and about 16 volunteers from Connecticut.

Their plan was to recruit additional men from the local Berkshire area and join forces with Colonel Ethan Allen and the Green Mountain Boys from Vermont.

The place where the meeting took place is marked in downtown Pittsfield between Park Square and the

Easton's Tavern

Near this spot stood Easton's Tavern. Here on May 1, 1775, Colonel James Easton and John Brown of Pittsfield and Captain Edward Mott of Preston, Connecticut planned the capture of Fort Ticonderoga which on May 10th surrendered to the Continental Volunteers under Ethan Allen with Colonel Easton second in command.

(Pittsfield Marker)

Berkshire Museum on the east side of US Route 7 (South Street). There is a stone marker where the meeting took place.

A little over two years after this meeting (August 14, 1777), word reached Pittsfield that British forces were advancing to seize Bennington's storehouses. A rally was held at the meeting house (not far from today's South Congregational Church) and troops were mustered. A company under the leadership of Captain William Ford included William Easton and the "Fighting Parson," Thomas Allen. A regiment under the leadership of Colonel Simonds and a detachment under the command of Lieutenant-Colonel David Rossiter of Richmond completed the forces. After a powerful address by Parson Allen, they left in haste for Bennington. An observer noted that the Parson chose to march to Bennington in his sulky, "wisely conserving his forces for combat."

The troops from the Berkshires were joined by troops from New Hampshire and Vermont. At the Battle of Bennington, they were able to secure a major victory against the British.

The sundial was first given by the Daughters of the American Revolution, 1903. Restored by Pittsfield High School student historians in 1992. The Pittsfield elm stood on this location from 1524 to 1864.

(Pittsfield Marker)

> Erected to the memory of Mr. & Mrs. John Chandler Williams who made possible this park. Mr. Williams gave this land. Mrs. Williams once saved the old elm from destruction, 1790.
>
>   (Pittsfield Marker)

A stone memorial at the Bennington Battlefield (an upcoming stop) notes the valuable service rendered by these patriotic volunteers.

Pittsfield's Park Square — Park Square is the center of Pittsfield where North Street, East Street, South Street and West Street all meet. Many historical markers can be found around the square.

At the middle of Park Square and for more than a century, including the Revolutionary War period, an

> On this spot, in the days of the Revolutionary War, stood "The Old Coffee House" where were kept many British Prisoners.
>
>   (Pittsfield Marker)

First Church of Christ in Pittsfield

Congregational, February 7, 1764.

(Pittsfield Marker)

old elm tree witnessed Pittsfield history. There are two markers in the square about the Old Elm.

On the south side of park square at the entrance to Patrick's Pub is a marker indicating that a Pittsfield coffee house was used here as a prison. At Bennington, American forces took 700 prisoners. No doubt, some of them spent time at this coffee house prison.

On this site was located the residence of

Parson Thomas Allen

Ordained the first congregational minister of Pittsfield, 1764. Served forty-six years. Chaplain in the Revolutionary Army. Active in the Battle of Bennington.

(Pittsfield Marker)

21

On the north side of Park Square is the First Church of Christ. The marker on the church indicates this congregation was active throughout the Revolution.

The northeast corner of Park Square was the site of Parson Allen's home. There is a marker at the location.

Breakfast in Pittsfield — Just east of the Parson Allen marker is the Court Square Breakfast & Deli, a great place to get your **Revolutionary Day** started.

While you're having breakfast there, remember that not far from this very spot on the 2nd of May, 1775, Edward Mott and the Connecticut volunteers and James Easton, John Brown and the Berkshire volunteers had breakfast before their march to Bennington.

PITTSFIELD TO WILLIAMSTOWN

Mile Mark 0.0 — Leave Pittsfield on East Street, bear left onto First Street which is US Route 7 heading north.

Mile Mark 3.0 — Travel along the east bank of Pontoosuc Lake. Watch for Mount Greylock, the tallest mountain in Massachusetts, in the distance.

Mile Mark 5.4 — Reach the center of Lanesboro. On the right side of US Route 7, there is a set of church stairs with a marker on top.

Mile Mark 6.5 — On the left side of US Route 7, one mile north of the center of Lanesboro, you will see St. Luke's Old Stone Church.

This tablet on the original steps of the marble from the Lanesboro Quarries marks the site of the first and second meeting house of the First Church of Christ in Lanesboro organized March 28, 1764.

"I have reared me a monument more lasting than bronze."

(Lanesboro Marker)

Although the church was built in 1835, the parish, which was formed in 1767, existed at the time of the Revolutionary War and was a likely recruiting stop on the way to Bennington.

Just past the church on the right is a road that goes to the summit of Mount Greylock. On the summit is a veterans memorial tower from which there is a breathtaking three-state view. The trip to the summit is recommended on a longer visit to the area.

Mile Mark 10.3 — On the left is Brodie Mountain Ski Area. Brodie is a popular winter resort that is very Irish. On St. Patrick's Day you can ski on green snow.

Mile Mark 16.0 — Detour from US Route 7 at South Williamstown Five Corners. Watch for the corner store on the right and the marker in front. Turn right onto

South Williamstown Five Corners

Site of first cabin built by Isaac Stratton in 1762; first tavern, built by Samuel Sloan in 1767; town meetings in second story hall built by John Jordan in early 1830's.

Erected by
Williamstown
Bicentennial Committee

(Williamstown Marker)

Massachusetts Route 43 going north. Route 43 is a more historic route along the river into Williamstown.

Don't mistake the street addresses for dates — these home don't originate from the 1500's.

Mile Mark 20.6 — Arrive in Williamstown

The northern part of the house is one of the earliest extant structures in town. Built about 1767 in regulation size, it was enlarged to become a saltbox. In the mid 1970's, it was enlarged to its present form.

(Williamstown Marker)

WILLIAMSTOWN

Williamstown was founded in 1753. Near the center of the town is the oldest home. It is at the corner of Water Street (Route 43) and Latham Street. In front of the home is a marker.

A few blocks further north on Water Street is the intersection with Massachusetts Route 2, the famous Mohawk Trail. The Mohawk Trail follows the old Native American trail originally used by the Mohawk Indians. The trail goes through the Berkshires to Boston and passes by the very important Revolutionary War towns of Lexington and Concord, but that's part of another **Revolutionary Day**.

The intersection at Water Street and Route 2 is also near the center of Williams College, which was founded in 1793. Just up the hill to the left, Route 2 intersects with US Route 7. At the intersection is a park

West College

Original Williams College building., completed in 1790 as a free school under bequest of Col. Ephraim Williams, killed at Battle of Lake George, Sept. 8, 1755, and for whom Williamstown is named. The free school became Williams College in 1793.

(Williamstown Marker)

that contains the 1753 House. The house was constructed for the Williamstown Bicentennial in 1953 with tools and materials used in 1753.

Also in the park is a meetinghouse marker. The first meetinghouse was likely visited on May 2, 1775 by the

> ## Site of the First Meeting House
>
> This park was the site of the first meeting house built in 1768 and removed in 1797 to make way for a second meeting house completed in 1798 and destroyed by fire on January 21, 1866.
>
> (Williamstown Marker)

patriot forces enroute to Ticonderoga. At the time of their visit, they consisted of:

- Edward Mott and about 16 volunteers from Connecticut
- James Easton, John Brown and the Berkshire volunteers they had recruited thus far in Pittsfield, Lanesboro and Hancock.

Additional men were recruited in Williamstown to join the Berkshire volunteers for the assault on Fort Ticonderoga.

The park was also the site of West Hoosic Fort used in the French and Indian War in 1756. There are two markers near the Williams Inn that recount the history of the fort and its defenders.

About a mile further north on Route 7 is a bridge across the Hoosic River. Just over the bridge on the left is the River Bend Farm Bed & Breakfast. In front of the B&B is a marker. The home was formerly owned by Colonel Simonds. A stone memorial at the

River Bend Farmhouse Tavern

Built about 1770 by Benjamin Simonds who was captured at Fort Massachusetts 1746, redeemed in 1747, soldier at the West Hoosic 1750-1756, first settler, 1752, father of the first child born in this town, colonel in the Revolutionary War and commander of the Massachusetts Forces at the Battle of Bennington.

(Williamstown Marker)

Bennington Battlefield (an upcoming stop) notes the valuable service rendered by the Massachusetts Forces under his command.

WILLIAMSTOWN TO OLD BENNINGTON

Mile Mark 22.5 — Continue traveling north along US Route 7

At the west of this marker lies the homestead farm of Peter Harwood, a member of the little band of pioneers who located in Vermont, June 18, 1761. He was father of Benjamin Harwood, the first child born in Bennington, and the house built by him in 1769 is incorporated in the residence directly opposite.

Placed by the National Society of the Colonial Dames of America in the State of Vermont, August 16, 1927.

(Bennington Marker)

Near this spot stood the first school house built in Bennington, August 1760. August 16, 1927 by the children of all the schools in the town of Bennington.

(Bennington Marker)

Mile Mark 23.7 — Cross the border between Massachusetts and Vermont. You are now traveling on the Ethan Allen Highway, named in his honor by the State of Vermont.

Mile Mark 28.7 — Travel through the town of Pownal Center -- a town once famous for its racetrack.

Mile Mark 32.7 — Reach the intersection with Carpenter Hill Road. Turn left and bear to the right, also the way to Southern Vermont College.

Mile Mark 33.3 — In the distance, there is a view of the Bennington Monument at Old Bennington.

Mile Mark 33.6 — Watch for the Peter Harwood marker on the left.

Mile Mark 33.8 — Reach a stop sign. Continue straight on Monument Avenue.

Parson Jedediah Dewey

c. 1763

(Bennington Marker)

Mile Mark 34.9 — The road splits as you arrive in Old Bennington. Although it seems a little unnatural, take the split to the left and try to find a parking spot before you reach Route 9. The roads around the Old Bennington common are a puzzle of one-way and two-way streets with a very busy Route 9 snaking its way through the middle. Taking the left split simplifies parking and access to Route 9. Note that there is a former parsonage near the split on the right a short distance from Old First Church.

Arrive in Old Bennington. Be sure to watch for the church groundhog during your visit.

OLD BENNINGTON

Old Bennington Commons — Much of the early history of Vermont took place in Old Bennington. In front of the Old First Church, on the commons, is a large marker in stone on the ground.

The church was first organized in 1762. As indicated by the markers in the area, it played a prominent role in Vermont's early history.

Old First Church, Vermont's Colonial Shrine

The Old First Church was gathered in 1762, the first Protestant church in Vermont. Much of the early history of Bennington and of Vermont took place in and around the original meeting house built in 1763 and the present church dedicated in 1806. As a result, the Vermont legislature in 1935 designated the church as Vermont's Colonial Shrine. Standing today, much as it did during its dedication in 1806, the church is one of the first beautiful examples of early colonial architecture. The cemetery adjacent to the church contains the graves of so many of the citizens who contributed so much to the founding of Bennington and Vermont. It also contains the graves of Robert Frost and approximately 75 revolutionary war patriots as well as British and Hessian Soldiers killed in the Battle of Bennington. The site of Ethan Allen's home is on the border of the cemetery.

(Bennington Monument Exhibit)

Vermont Freedom and Unity
for God and for Country

The first protestant church in the present limits of Vermont was organized here, December 3, 1762, the settlers having arrived June 18, 1761. On this site was erected in 1763-1765 the first meeting house in the New Hampshire Grants, a plain building of unpainted wood, 50 feet by 40 feet, replaced in 1806 by the present church edifice. Here preached Jedediah Dewey, the first minister of the church, the trusted counselor of the colonists. Here the forefathers met in prayer for assistance against the oppressive measures of New York and the overwhelming power of King George. Hither, the settlers returned from the capture of Ticonderoga, the Battle of Bennington, the surrender of Burgoyne to offer up their thanksgiving and here were brought the 700 prisoners captured on August 16, 1777. For forty years, the center of the religious life of the community, the meeting house was also connected with the political life of the state. Vermont was an independent republic from January 17, 1777 to its admission into the union, March 4, 1791. The first legislature met at Windsor in 1778 and adjourned to Bennington for its June session held on this site. The laws for the carrying on the government for this sovereign state were enacted at the session of the

(Continued on page 35)

(Continued from page 34)

legislature which assembled in the meeting house, February 11, 1779. Here met the convention consisting of one delegate from each town, which on January 10, 1791 ratified the constitution of the United States by the signatures of 105 out of 109 delegates, thereby preparing the way for the admission of Vermont into the Union as the first state after the original thirteen.

(Bennington Marker)

The graveyard behind the church contains the graves of about 75 revolutionary war patriots as well as British and Hessian Soldiers killed in the Battle of Bennington. The grave of American Poet, Robert Frost, is also in the cemetery.

Around this stone lie buried many patriots who fell in the Battle of Bennington, August 16, 1777. Here also rests British soldiers and Hessians who died from wounds after the battle. As captives, they were confined in the first meeting house building which stood on the green west of this burying ground.

(Bennington Marker)

Behind the cemetery is the Bennington Museum The museum contains many artifacts from the revolutionary war period including the Bennington Battle flag, which is thought to be oldest stars and stripes in existence. There are also uniforms, firearms and early tools. The museum entrance is just off Route 9 East.

At the southeast corner of the intersection of Route 9 and Monument Avenue near the graveyard that surrounds Old First Church is a stone marker indicating the place where Ethan Allen's home once stood. Inside the cemetery, there is a memorial stone for those who fought at the Battle of Bennington.

Across the street from the church is the Walloomsac Inn. The former inn was the oldest in the state, built in 1764. You might find a not-so-welcoming sign on the door: "This is a private home, it is no longer an inn. Please stay off the porch and property."

Vermont Molly Stark Trail and Historic Old Bennington

State Highway 9 traverses scenic Hogback Mountain to the Connecticut River valley. Old Bennington, site of the Battle Monument and Historical Museum was the meeting place of the Green Mountain Boys. It was the first town chartered by Governor Benning Wentworth of New Hampshire, in 1749.

(Bennington Museum Marker)

A few feet south from this stone stood the house where Ethan Allen lived while he was a resident of Bennington, 1769-1775.

(Bennington Marker)

Walloomsac Inn

Built in 1764, the inn is the oldest in the state. Many great dignitaries including Thomas Jefferson and James Madison stayed here.

(Bennington Monument Exhibit)

Catamount Tavern — About halfway up Monument Avenue from the church on the right is a marker for the Catamount Tavern, where the patriots would meet. At the time of their meeting, the patriot forces consisted of:

Ethan Allen's Route to Ticonderoga

3 May 1775 — Troops reach Bennington where Ethan Allen joins them for a council.

4 May 1775 — Ethan Allen leaves to muster the Green Mountain Boys.

5 May 1775 — Ethan Allen rejoins the group accompanied by Seth Warner.

(Fort Ticonderoga Exhibit)

- Edward Mott and about 16 volunteers from Connecticut
- James Easton, John Brown and about 40 men recruited from the Berkshires

They met on May 3rd with Ethan Allen at the Catamount Tavern. Edward Mott discussed their plan to seize badly needed cannon and munitions from the British for the defense of Boston. Ethan Allen, who was already considering a similar plan against the British, had garnered inside information about the fort and its contents. Over the

Brigadier General John Stark

1728 — 1822

Victor of the Battle At Bennington, 1777

"There they are boys! We beat them today or Molly Stark sleeps a widow tonight!"

Design by John Rogers - 1889
Sculpture by Robert Shure
Gift of John Brooks Threlfall - 1999

(Bennington Marker)

General Burgoyne's camp cooking kettle captured at Saratoga by the Americans, October 23, 1777.

Bennington Battle Monument

On August 16, 1777, British forces sent by General Burgoyne to seize supplies in Bennington were turned back by New Englanders under General John Stark and Vermont's Colonel Seth Warner. This 306 foot commemorative shaft planned 100 years later was dedicated in 1891. In 1953, it was taken over, restored, and an elevator installed by the Vermont Historic Site Commission, which now administers it for the state.

(Bennington Marker)

> On this site stood the Continental storehouse, object of the British attack that was repulsed by the Colonial forces at the Battle of Bennington, August 16, 1777.
>
> The expedition led by Lt. Col. Baum sent to seize military stores here was defeated by volunteer American Militia Forces from New Hampshire, Massachusetts and Vermont commanded by General John Stark aided by Colonels Warner and Herrick of Vermont, Simonds of Massachusetts, and Nichols of New Hampshire.
>
> (Bennington Marker)

next two days, he mustered two hundred Green Mountain Boys and took command of the operation. On May 5th, the group left for Castleton where Benedict Arnold would join their group and final plans would be made.

Bennington Battle Monument — At the top of Monument Avenue is the Bennington Battle Monument. This 306-foot shaft, dedicated in 1891, commemorates the Battle of Bennington. An elevator takes you up to the center of the monument where there is a 360-degree view of the Bennington area. To the south is Old Bennington. To the west, in the distance, is the Bennington Battlefield, although you can't

New Hampshire at the Battle of Bennington

Erected in honor of Brigadier General John Stark and the 1400 New Hampshire men who came to the defense of Vermont in August 17, 1777. Assembling at Fort No. 4 in Charleston, New Hampshire, Stark and his troops crossed the Green Mountains to aid in the defense of the newly established State of Vermont. As the commander and chief of all the American Forces from New Hampshire, Vermont, Massachusetts and New York, General Stark had approximately 2,000 men in all. In the first phase of the battle, General Stark's army defeated and captured a British detachment led by Lieutenant Colonel Friedrick Baum. Shortly after this triumph with the timely assistance of Colonel Seth Warner and his Green Mountain Boys, a relief column under Colonel Heindrick Von Breymann was repulsed. By thus denying the enemy sorely needed supplies, these twin victories near Bennington on August 16, 1777 contributed notably to the total British surrender at Saratoga two months later and to the subsequent military alliance with France, the turning point in the War for American Independence.

(Bennington Marker)

John Stark by Alonzo Chappel

Colonel Seth Warner

Colonel Warner with the Green Mountain Boys won a decisive victory over the British reinforcements in the second engagement at Bennington, August 16, 1777. Thus saving the military stores at that place crippling Burgoyne's army so as to stop his invading march and establishing a turning point in the War of the American Revolution.

Born in Roxbury, CT, then Woodbury, CT, May 17, 1743, resided in Bennington, VT, 1765-1784, died December 26, 1784 at Roxbury, CT where he was buried with honors of war, aged 41.

Commander of the Green Mountain Boys in battles at Breckenridge Farms, July and October 1771; Otter Creek Falls, 1778; Capture of Crown Point, May 11, 1775; At Longuel and in the invasion of Canada, 1775; Hubbardton, July 7, 1777; Bennington, August 16, 1777; and Continental Service, 1778-1780.

An able statesman and soldier, he assisted the people of Vermont to establish their independence and to organize an independent state government under which they existed for a period of 14 years when the state was admitted to the Federal Union and during the Revolutionary War aided the 13 Colonies in acquiring their independence.

"Tell future ages what a hero has done." This memorial was erected by Colonel Olin Scott, Bennington, 1910.

(Bennington Marker)

actually see it from the monument.

On the north side of the monument is a statue of General John Stark. On the south side is a statue of Colonel Seth Warner.

The Bennington Monument is on the site of the Continental storehouses that were the objective of the British attack on August 16, 1777.

OLD BENNINGTON TO THE BENNINGTON BATTLEFIELD

Mile Mark 35.4 — From the parking lot at the battle monument, go around the rotary in a clockwise direction (the rotary is a two-way street). Pass Monument Avenue and go straight onto Walloomsac Road. About a mile down the road, you will see the airport on the right.

Mile Mark 36.6 — Go past the entrance to the airport and turn right onto Whipstock Road.

Mile Mark 38.4 — On the right, there is a Harmon Tavern marker.

Continue on Whipstock Road for another two-tenths of a mile and turn left onto Austin Hill. About a half-mile down Austin Hill, you will see Bennington College in the distance.

Mile Mark 39.4 — Reach a stop sign. Turn left onto Murphy Road.

Two hundred feet west of this marker stood the tavern of Captain Daniel Harmon, built about 1771. General John Stark had breakfast in the tavern August 14, 1777. Daniel Williams Harmon, noted Canadian explorer, was born in the tavern, February 19, 1778.

The marker was erected by the Bennington Battlefield Monument and Historical Association, 1950.

(Bennington Marker)

Birthplace of Vermont

Near this site stood the homestead of Lieutenant James Breckenridge. After years of peaceable possession, his farm was claimed by New York land speculators. A sheriff and over 300 men came from Albany to evict him from his home. Aided by men from Bennington, a brave defense was made without bloodshed proving to be a declaration of the independence of the state of Vermont, July 19, 1771.

The home of four generations was destroyed by fire in 1889.

(Bennington Marker)

Mile Mark 39.7 — Watch for the "Birth of Vermont" marker on the right that stands in the middle of the front yard of a Bennington home.

This marker tells us that the people of Vermont were fighting for independence from not only Britain, but also from New York. The fight for independence from New York actually began in Albany, New York in June of 1770 when Ethan Allen was thrown out of court for not having "admissible evidence" from which to make a case. New York would not recognize the legality of deeds to land currently owned in the New Hampshire Grants (as Vermont was called at the time).

Vermont made many attempts to get recognition as an independent colony in Congress - all blocked by a very powerful New York, but supported by New Hampshire and the other New England colonies. In 1777, Vermont boldly declared itself an independent republic. For fourteen years, Vermont had its own national capital, its own money and its own militia[1]. Congress finally admitted Vermont as the 14th state in 1791.

Although most of the sparring with New York produced little bloodshed, the exception was the "Westminster Massacre." On March 13, 1775, a provoked New York Sheriff and his posse fired into a courthouse filled with unarmed protesting Vermonters. Many were wounded and two Vermonters were killed as a result of the incident. They were Daniel Houghton[2] and William French (to whom this book is dedicated). There is a monument in Westminster that honors these Vermonters who gave their lives for Vermont independence.

The Westminster Massacre polarized Vermonters and helped to fill the ranks of the Green Mountain Boys for the defense of Vermont. Two months after the massacre, they would agree that the British posed a

Forty feet west of this marker stood the home of Seth Warner. Colonel of the Green Mountain Boys during his residence in Bennington, hero of Hubbardton and Bennington battles, 1777. The house was destroyed by fire in 1858.

(Bennington Marker)

bigger threat and marched to Fort Ticonderoga for the defense of Boston.

Mark 40.4 — Continue up the road just two-tenths of a mile and you will find a Seth Warner marker in the front yard of another Vermont home.

A short distance further up the road is one of Vermont's famous covered bridges. Next to the bridge is a marker.

Across the street from the bridge is the Henry House Inn B&B. Above the door of the inn is the year, 1769.

The Henry Covered Bridge
Across the Walloomsac River

This quiet spot was once a major river crossing. Traffic between southwestern Vermont and New York State crossed here until a railroad was built in 1852.

Troops marched from Manchester, Vermont to the Battle of Bennington in 1777 and teams and stages transported freight and passengers.

The original Henry Covered Bridge was built in 1840. In the 1860's and 1870's, heavy wagonloads of iron-ore were hauled over the bridge from the Burden Iron Company Mine on Orebed Road to its washing works on Paran Creek in North Bennington.

A succession of water-powered mills was located next to the bridge on the south side. The last was a gristmill operated into the 1920's by Burtine T. Henry, one of this area's many descendants of the Irish Born, William Henry, 1734-1811.

This bridge is supported by town lattice trusses. The design patented in 1820 by Connecticut architect Ithiel Town represented a great technological leap forward from the earlier heavy timber, king post and queen post, and burr truss styles. Carpenters with saws and drills could assemble a lighter, stronger, web-like truss from mill-sawn planks secured with wooden pegs. Bridges were covered to protect the structural skeleton from moisture, helping to protect the bridge.

This bridge, built in 1989 by the State of Vermont Agency of Transportation, is a replica replacing the deteriorating original bridge built in 1840. Two other

(Continued on page 50)

> *(Continued from page 49)*
>
> covered bridges, the Paper Mill Village covered bridge and the Silk Road covered bridge cross the Walloomsac River within two miles upstream.
>
> (Bennington Marker)

Before crossing the bridge, be sure to check the other side for oncoming traffic. The bridge only supports traffic in one direction. After the crossing the bridge, turn left onto Harrington Road.

Mile Mark 41.1 — Don't Panic! Harrington Road becomes a hard-packed dirt road.

Mile Mark 41.7 — Watch for a Stark marker in the yard on the side of a Vermont home. Stark's famous quote appears on the marker, but in a briefer form than the one on the marker at the Bennington Monument.

Mile Mark 42.5 — Reach a stop sign. Turn left at the intersection. You are now traveling west on Vermont Route 67.

Mile Mark 42.7 — Two-tenths of a mile past the stop sign is a Baum marker on the right.

> **General John Stark's Camping Ground**
> **August 14-15-16, 1777**
>
> "There are the Redcoats and they are ours, or this night Molly Stark sleeps a widow."
>
> (Bennington Marker)

A few feet east of this marker stood the house, removed about 1870, in which Lieutenant Colonel Friedrich Baum died. Commander of the enemy forces, he was mortally wounded in the battle of Bennington and died two days later, August 18, 1777. He was buried on the north bank of the Walloomsac River west of this site. The precise spot not now being known.

(Bennington Marker)

Mile Mark 43.1 — Cross the border into New York. About a mile and half past the border, Route 67 begins to hug the south side of a mountain. This is the mountain on which the battle of Bennington took place.

Mile Mark 44.9 — Reach the entrance to the Bennington Battlefield. The site's hours are posted as 10AM - 6PM, weekends only, but they are open on weekdays in the summer time.

---

1. Remnants of the Vermont Militia can still be found today at Norwich University in Northfield, Vermont. As an undergraduate, the author was taught history by a commissioned officer from the Vermont Militia. These commissions are provided to Norwich administrators and

faculty, if needed, so that they may participate as officers in Norwich's Military College of Vermont. It is a thrilling, weekend sight for any Vermont history buff to see the Corps of Cadet's parade in front of the President of Norwich University, who, today, is the highest ranking officer in the Vermont Militia. Norwich University was founded in 1819 and is the birthplace of the Reserve Officer's Training Corps (ROTC).

2. Ralph and John Houghton, who were cousins, came to Lancaster, Massachusetts from Eaton Bray in England around 1649. Descendants, including the family of Daniel Houghton, moved into the southern Vermont area in the early to mid 1700's and still remain there today. The author, also a descendant, was born in Greenfield, Massachusetts just south of his father's birthplace, Brattleboro, Vermont.

Bennington Battlefield
General Stark's Victory
August 16, 1777
(Battlefield Marker)

BENNINGTON BATTLEFIELD

At the entrance to the battlefield, there is a marker. Inside the gates, there is a very narrow road through a heavily wooded area that climbs to the summit of a hill. At the top of the hill, there are three stone memorials, other markers, a relief map showing the battlefield area and a parking area.

> **Battle of Bennington**
> **First Engagement**
> **August 16, 1777**
>
> General John Stark with New Hampshire, Vermont, and Massachusetts' militia defeated and captured an expeditionary force sent by General Burgoyne and commanded by Colonel Baum. This was one of the first decisive victories in the War of the Revolution.
>
> (Battlefield Marker)

Bennington Battlefield — Some of the markers indicate battlefield positions including those of Colonel Nichol's New Hampshire Regiment and Colonel Herrick's Vermont Rangers. There is one stone memorial for each of the participating states.

> A memorial commemorating the record of New Hampshire troops under the command of John Stark in this important and decisive engagement, August 16, 1777.
>
> (Battlefield Marker)

Bennington Battlefield

By the end of July 1777, the British invasion from Canada under General John Burgoyne had progressed to Fort Edward on the Hudson River. Desperately in need of supplies, Burgoyne, on August 11th dispatched an expedition under Lieutenant Colonel Friedrick Baum to capture the American storehouse at Bennington, VT, which were thought to be guarded by only a handful of rebel militia. About half of Baum's troops were mercenaries who only spoke German. Although from Brunswick, these men, like all German troops, were commonly called Hessians by the Americans. The rest of Baum's forces consisted of smaller detachments of British sharpshooters, Indians, Canadians and American Loyalists. The British, however, grossly underestimated American strength. New Hampshire had raised over 1,500 under General John Stark to meet Burgoyne's threat. An additional militia from Vermont and Western Massachusetts also turned out. Aware that the American resistance was growing, Baum, on August 14th, encamped his troops on and around this hill, just five miles from Bennington to await reinforcements. On August 16th, following a day of rain, Stark deployed his troops to attack Baum from all sides. In a two-hour battle, Baum's outposts collapsed and the main redoubt atop this hill was overrun, but not before Baum's

(Continued on page 56)

(Continued from page 55)

dragoons gamely fought off the attackers with their sabers. Too late to help Baum, reinforcements under Lieutenant Heindrick von Breymann approached from the west, only to driven off by Seth Warner's Vermont Militia. Baum was killed in the battle as were 200 hundred of his men and all but a few of the remainder became American prisoners. "Wherever the King's Forces point, militia to the amount of 3,000 or 4,000 assemble in 24 hours," a frustrated Burgoyne wrote to his superiors after the defeat. "Vermont has to contain the most rebellious race on the continent and hangs like a gathering storm upon my left." Americans made their stand at Saratoga where Burgoyne, his army weakened by dwindling supplies, surrendered on October 17, 1777.

(Battlefield Monument)

Erected here by the Commonwealth of Massachusetts as a tribute to her patriotic volunteers who rendered valuable service in the repulse of the Burgoyne invasion at the Battle of Bennington, August 16, 1777.

(Battlefield Marker)

In grateful memory of the patriots of Vermont and of their fellow patriots of the neighboring states who here fought for American Independence under the command of General John Stark and Colonel Seth Warner, August 16, 1777.

(Battlefield Marker)

Battle of Bennington
by Alonzo Chappel

Bennington Battlefield, Second Engagement — About a mile west, past the entrance to the battlefield, on Route 67 is the town of Walloomsac, NY. Across the street from the Walloomsac home (1843) and to the right side of a local restaurant, there is a marker for the second engagement.

Battle of Bennington

Second Engagement

August 16, 1777

At this point occurred the defeat of Colonel Breymann who commanded a force of 600 men sent by General Burgoyne to reinforce Colonel Baum. Colonel Seth Warner and his regiment of Vermont Rangers and Green Mountain Boys distinguished themselves in this action.

(Battlefield Marker)

BENNINGTON BATTLEFIELD TO ARLINGTON

Mile Mark 47.2 — From the town of Walloomsac, travel east on New York 67 back toward the Bennington Battlefield.

Mile Mark 50.2 — Cross the state border once again.

Mile Mark 52.1 — Reach the center of North Bennington and an intersection with Vermont 67A. Bear left just before the railroad tracks and continue on Vermont 67 East.

Mile Mark 52.5 — At a stop sign, turn right and continue east on Vermont 67.

Mile Mark 54.1 — Reach an unmarked split in the road, bear left.

Mile Mark 54.4 — Reach the intersection with Historic Route 7A (old US Route 7). Turn left on Route 7A heading north. Although US Route 7 is a faster way to Manchester, it is not nearly as scenic.

Mile Mark 56.7 — Travel though the town of Shaftsbury.

Mile Mark 63.8 — As you approach the town of Arlington, the mountain that you see in the distance is Mount Equinox. It is 3,835 feet above sea level, the highest mountain in the Taconic range that runs south of Rutland.

As you enter Arlington, look for the marker declaring it the capital of Vermont in 1787. Since we know at this time Vermont was an independent republic, Arlington was once a nation's capital.

Arrive at the main intersection at the center of Arlington.

Vermont Seal from Bennington, Vermont

Chittendon Home

Oldest frame building, one block east built by Jehiel Hawley, 1764, was home of Thomas Chittendon, Vermont's first governor. Legend says that the western vista with its great pine became the state seal in 1779. Ethan and Ira Allen lived nearby.

(Arlington Marker)

ARLINGTON

At the northeast corner of Arlington's main intersection is a home with a Governor Chittendon marker in front. A block east of the home is the Masonic Temple with historic markers on each side. Missing from the markers is the fact that sometime around May 6th, 1775, the patriot forces consisting of:

- Edward Mott and about 16 volunteers from Connecticut
- James Easton, John Brown and about 40 volunteers from the Berkshires.

> Near this spot stood the residence occupied during part of the conflict for the American Independence by Thomas Chittendon, first governor of Vermont and one of the principle founders of the commonwealth.
>
> (Arlington Marker)

- Ethan Allen, Seth Warner and about 200 Green Mountain Boys

passed through the area on their way to Ticonderoga.

> Near this spot stood the residence occupied during part of the conflict for the American Independence by Ethan Allen, resolute leader of the Green Mountain Boys whose courageous deeds in spoken and written words contributed powerfully to the establishment of the independent state of Vermont. He led the first successful, aggressive military expedition of the American Revolution when he captured Ticonderoga.
>
> (Arlington Marker)

On the main street, just a few buildings up from the Chittendon Home marker, is an art gallery with paintings from another of Arlington's famous residents, Norman Rockwell.

Before continuing north on Route 7A, look to the west and see if you can see the "western vista with its great pine" that inspired the seal of Vermont. Today, it looks like the pine has been replaced by a maple. Given the importance of Vermont's maple sugar industry, the change may be appropriate.

ARLINGTON TO MANCHESTER

Mile Mark 64.0 — Depart Arlington.

Mile Mark 67.5 — Reach the Ira Allen House B&B. In front of the house is a marker.

> "It is to be remembered that this was the first offensive part taken against Great Britain in the American Revolution,"
>
> - Ira Allen, 1798 (referring to the capture of Fort Ticonderoga).

Sunderland
Allen Families Lived Here

Ira Allen lived on this site by the Battenkill and as treasurer and surveyor general, his office helped to shape the destiny of the republic of Vermont.

Here, Ethan's family lived. Here, he dictated his free-thinking oracles of reason in 1782. To his bride, his second wife, he presented the first copy.

(Sunderland Marker)

Mile Mark 68.0 — Reach the road to the summit of Mount Equinox. The trip to the summit takes about a half hour and is a recommended stop on a longer visit to the area.

Mile Mark 70.9 — Pass the Seth Warner Inn on the left.

Mile Mark 71.4 — Pass Hildene, the former mansion-home of Robert Todd Lincoln, Abraham Lincoln's surviving son. The mansion was built in 1904 and is also a recommended stop on a longer visit to the area.

Mile Mark 72.1 — Arrive in Manchester.

MANCHESTER

In the center of Manchester is a veterans memorial. At the top of the memorial is a statue of a Green Mountain Boy. Across the street from the memorial is The Equinox, one of Vermont's best and largest resort hotels.

Manchester was a revolutionary crossroad in 1775 and 1777. Around May 6, 1775, it was visited by the patriot forces consisting of:

- Edward Mott and about 16 volunteers from Connecticut.
- James Easton, John Brown and about 40 volunteers from the Berkshires.
- Ethan Allen, Seth Warner and about 200 Green Mountain Boys.

They marched through Manchester on their way to Castleton to make plans for the capture of Fort Ticonderoga.

On July 9, 1777, Manchester was a much different kind of revolutionary crossroad. About 2,500 retreating Americans under the command of Major General Arthur St. Clair passed through Manchester on a long circuitous route that began at Fort Ticonderoga on July

5th. The retreat started after superior British forces began moving artillery up nearby Mount Defiance. The Americans crossed Lake Champlain to Mount Independence on a floating bridge, then destroyed the bridge after crossing. They evacuated Mount Independence and traveled down the military road through Hubbardton. There, a pursuing British detachment was halted by American forces. The rest of  the Americans continued their retreat through Castleton then east (along today's US Route 4) to Rutland so they would avoid meeting the British at Skenesborough (today's Whitehall). They marched south (along today's Route 7A) to Manchester, then trekked southwest, paralleling the Battenkill River, to Fort Miller. This completed a journey of about 100 miles.

They arrived at Fort Miller on July 12th, hungry, exhausted, poorly clothed and totally disorganized. Under the leadership of General Philip Schuyler, they recovered, moved south to Saratoga, regrouped, reorganized and began preparation to meet the British forces moving south from Skenesborough. About a month later, Burgoyne arrived at Fort Miller with British forces numbering about 8,000. Shortly after their arrival, Burgoyne launched the fateful expedition to Bennington to obtain horses and supplies. On September 13th, Burgoyne would leave Fort Miller to be defeated by an American Army that was approaching 20,000 at the Battles of Saratoga. This was the "turning point" of the American Revolution.

After the Battle of Hubbardton, Seth Warner and the Green Mountain Boys retreated over the mountains toward Rutland and regrouped here in Manchester at an encampment just behind the Equinox. In August, they would break camp and march south to participate in the Battle of Bennington.

MANCHESTER TO RUTLAND

Mile Mark 72.1 — Leave Manchester going north on Route 7A, but watch your speed. The limit is 30 mph for the next couple miles.

Mile Mark 72.9 — As you approach Manchester Center, you'll begin to notice one of the reasons this area is popular -- brand-name shopping. You'll find one store for every brand name, e.g., Danz, Seiko, Nautica, Boze, Tommy Hilfiger, Jockey, Calvin Klein, Van Husen, Godiva, Timberland. Careful, there are pedestrians all over the place.

Mile Mark 78.1 — Route 7A meets US Route 7 after passing though the village of Dorset. Turn left onto US Route 7 and take the high-speed route into Rutland.

Mile Mark 95.0 — Travel through the town of Wallingford. For the next ten miles, US Route 7 gradually opens up to a four lane split highway, indistinguishable from an interstate.

Mile Mark 98.3 — As you pass by the town of Clarendon, watch for a brief glimpse of Killington Mountain off to the right in the distance. If you look

carefully, you can see a building on the side of the mountain that is the top of the gondola lift.

Mile Mark 102.7 — You'll know you're approaching the center of Rutland when everything comes to a full stop. And then after inching forward to the next intersection, everything comes to a stop again, and again, and again ... As you crawl into the center of Rutland, you'll notice plenty of opportunities for lunch, e.g., Ponderosa Steakhouse, Denny's, Friendly's, Sirloin Saloon, McDonald's, KFC, Dunkin' Donuts, Midway Diner, Wendy's, Burger King. But you might want to wait — there's a great little outdoor restaurant on the other side of Rutland.

Mile Mark 104.9 — Reach a park on the left. You have reached the center of Rutland.

Green Mountain Boys

Erected by the Ann Storey Chapter, Daughters of the American Revolution. 1915.

(Rutland Marker)

RUTLAND

The monument to the Green Mountain Boys is in the center of a beautiful, peaceful park, surrounded by flowers.

Like Manchester, Rutland was also a revolutionary crossroad for the Green Mountain Boys. Around May 7, 1775, it was visited by the patriot force consisting of:

- Edward Mott and about 16 volunteers from Connecticut.
- James Easton, John Brown and about 40 volunteers from the Berkshires.
- Ethan Allen, Seth Warner and about 200 Green Mountain Boys.

The force marched through Rutland on their way to Castleton to make plans for the capture of Fort Ticonderoga.

On July 8, 1777, Rutland was a temporary safe-haven for Major General Arthur St. Clair and 2,500 retreating American troops. It would later be a refuge for the Green Mountain Boys who had escaped over the mountains from the Battle of Hubbardton.

Just up US Route 7 from the park is the intersection with US Route 4 Business. At the northeast corner of this busy intersection is a Fort Rutland marker.

Fort Rutland, 1775

Erected on the site of Fort Rutland by the Ann Storey Chapter, Daughters of the American Revolution, June 14, 1901.

(Rutland Marker)

RUTLAND TO CASTLETON

Mile Mark 104.9 — From Rutland, begin a 90-mile detour from US Route 7 that will take you along the same route taken by Ethan Allen and General Arthur St. Clair. Take US Route 4 Business going west.

In downtown Rutland, US Route 4 Business loops around some of the congestion. Watch for the right turn and the two lefts.

Mile Mark 106.4 — Watch for the New Village Snack Bar on the right — a great local outdoor restaurant for  lunch. The menu includes some local specials like French fries with gravy, whole belly clams, and several versions of their chicken sandwich. The restaurant has picnic tables in a large picnic area in the back with both covered and uncovered tables

Across the street are the tracks for the Ethan Allen Express. This is the popular Amtrak ski train from New York City to Rutland. Busses take vacationers to the ski areas from Rutland.

Mile Mark 107.3 — When you cross the bridge over Otter Creek, watch for the waterfall on the right. Just after the bridge on the left is a marker for Mead's Falls.

Meade's Falls

James Meade, Rutland's first settler arrived at these falls on Otter Creek in 1769. The next year, he and his family were given shelter by members of the Caughnawag Tribe while they finished their log cabin. Meade built saw and gristmills on the falls and ran a ferry on Otter Creek. He was an ardent defender of the New Hampshire Grants and served as a Colonel in the militia. Mead's falls was an important military site. The 1759 Crown Point Military Road ran by here. General Arthur St. Clair wrote his report after the Battle of Hubbardton in 1777 at Mead's home on West Proctor Road. Fort Ranger was built in 1778 on the bluff northeast of the falls.

(Rutland Marker)

Mile Mark 107.7 — US Route 4 Business ends at the intersection with US Route 4 and Route 4A (Old US Route 4). Take Route 4A west.

Mile Mark 109.2 — Pass through the picturesque town of West Rutland and continue along curvy Route 4A, past hills, mountains and through a valley to Castleton.

Mile Mark 115.4 — As you near Castleton, watch for the intersection with East Hubbardton Road on the right and two markers in the northwest corner of the

intersection. East Hubbardton Road was part of the old military road to Fort Ticonderoga and Crown Point.

Fort Warren

Battle of Hubbardton, 7 Miles North

Directly east is the elevation for Fort Warren built in 1779 for defense of the Northern Frontier. The road from the north was the route of American retreat before Burgoyne protected by Colonel Seth Warner's rear guard action at the Battle of Hubbardton, July 7, 1777.

(Castleton Marker)

> **Conflict**
>
> **Site of Fort Warren, 1777-1779**
>
> Erected under the auspices Ann Storey Chapter, Daughters of the American Revolution, 1904.
>
> (Castleton Marker)

Both markers indicate that Fort Warren stood on this site from 1777-1779. After the loss of Fort Ticonderoga and Mount Independence, Fort Rutland, Fort Ranger and Fort Warren were part of a string of forts for the defense of Vermont. North of these forts all the way to Canada became a *demilitarized zone*. Those that entered or remained in the area did so at their own risk.

Mile Mark 116.0 — Arrive at Castleton.

Ethan Allen's Route to Ticonderoga

7 May 1775 — Entire contingent reaches Castleton, Vermont, and holds a council of war. Ethan Allen chosen commander of the expedition.

8 May 1775 — Ethan Allen marches northward.

9 May 1775 — On this day Benedict Arnold, accompanied by his manservant, joins the group and demands command of the expedition.

(Fort Ticonderoga Exhibit)

CASTLETON

The contingent of patriot forces now numbering over 250 soldiers consisted of:

- Edward Mott and about 16 volunteers from Connecticut.
- James Easton, John Brown and about 40 volunteers from the Berkshires.
- Ethan Allen, Seth Warner and about 200 Green Mountain Boys.

The patriot forces were here to make final plans to seize artillery and munitions from the British at Fort Ticonderoga for the defense of Boston. On May 9th,

Marking the meeting place of Ethan Allen and Benedict Arnold on their historic march to Fort Ticonderoga, May 9, 1775.

(Castleton Marker)

Colonel Benedict Arnold along with his manservant came with a commissioning from the Massachusetts Committee of Safety. He planned to use this official document to gain control of the operation.

The place of their meeting is marked near the congregational church. There is a marker in front of a patriotically decorated home behind the marker. The marker is on a metal plate embedded in stone and is very close to violating a supposed Federal Law. The law forbids the etching of Arnold's name in stone. This, of course, is due to Arnold's traitorous acts. Many believe he felt compelled to betray America because he was completely against any alliance with the French, an alliance that, ironically, he helped to create as a leader and hero at the Battle of Saratoga. But without a doubt, a traitor he was — he sought to deliver West Point to the British for 20,000 English pounds; in Virginia, he commanded British forces against American troops he once led; and later terrorized and burned New London, Connecticut in September, 1781.

Despite Benedict Arnold's efforts to take control of the expedition to Fort Ticonderoga, Ethan Allen and the Green Mountain Boys clearly made up the bulk of the forces. Allen, in his narrative, makes no mention of Arnold's participation in the attack.

> "...directions were privately sent to me from the then colony of Connecticut, to raise the Green Mountain Boys; with them to surprise and take the fortress Ticonderoga. This enterprise I cheerfully undertook; ..."
>
> — Ethan Allen, 1779

CASTLETON TO THE HUBBARDTON BATTLEFIELD

Mile Mark 117.2 — Return to the Fort Warren Marker and turn left onto East Hubbardton Road. Head up this old military road to the Hubbardton Battlefield. In the 1700's, this road was used by the Americans to get back and forth from Mount Independence and Fort Ticonderoga on Lake Champlain.

Mile Mark 117.4 — Crossover over US Route 4 and continue going north.

Mile Mark 121.8 — There are no markers between Castleton and the Hubbardton Battlefield, but there should be one about two miles south of the battlefield. It is here where General St. Clair and his forces were encamped when they heard gunshots that marked the beginning of the Battle of Hubbardton. It was the early morning hours of July 7, 1777. They broke camp quickly and were in Castleton just a few hours later.

East Hubbardton road becomes Monument Hill Road as you approach the battlefield. As you climb the road you will reach an open field on the top of the hill.

Mile Mark 123.8 — Arrival at Hubbardton Battlefield.

HUBBARDTON BATTLEFIELD

The Visitor Center is open from 9:30 AM to 5:30 PM. The center contains a museum and a three-dimensional relief map with fiber optics.

Walking Trail – The battlefield area is encircled by a walking trail that is about a half-mile in length. Along the trail are several markers that describe the battle and mark positions of the American and British Forces.

The Battle of Hubbardton – American Major General Arthur St. Clair, retreating from Fort Ticonderoga and Mount Independence, had left at Hubbardton about 1000 men to form a rear guard. Through this maneuver, St. Clair was not only able to escape after the British arrived with his weary and tattered main army, but he also stopped the pursuing forces in their tracks.

The American forces at Hubbardton were comprised of Vermont's Colonel Seth Warner with a detachment of Green Mountain Boys; a detail of Massachusetts militia under Colonel Ebenezer Francis; and Colonel Nathan Hale commanding the 2nd New Hampshire Continental Regiment.

The pursuing British units of Lieutenant General John Burgoyne's Army were seasoned regulars. Some 850

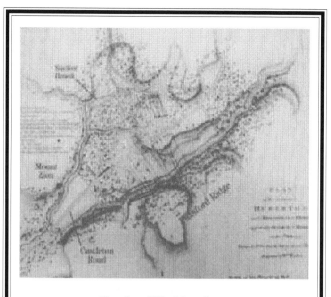

Battle of Hubbardton

Only battlefield on Vermont soil. Here on July 7, 1777 a successful rear guard action by Col. Seth Warner's Vermont, Massachusetts, and New Hampshire troops ended British pursuit under General Fraser and Riedesel. Thus General St. Clair's American Army retreating from Fort Ticonderoga and Mount Independence was saved to fight again near Bennington and Saratoga. Burgoyne's 1777 drive to divide the colonies first resisted at Hubbardton ended in defeat at Saratoga.

(Hubbardton Marker)

men were led by Brigadier General Simon Fraser, one of Burgoyne's best line officers. Fraser was ably supported by a detachment of 200 or so Brunswick troops under Major General Baron von Riedesel, a competent field officer.

About dawn, on the morning of the Battle, the stage was set: The British pursued the retreating Americans along the old military road from Mount Independence to Hubbardton. The course of the road is still clearly

Welcome to the Battle of Hubbardton State Historic Site

The only battle fought on Vermont Soil during the American Revolution took place on these fields. Viewed as a rearguard action, this battle was important because it slowed the progress of British and German pursuit long enough for the main body of the American Army to escape during their retreat from Fort Ticonderoga and Mount Independence on Lake Champlain. Starting from where you are now, follow the path to your right to the crest of the hill. There you will find the first of a series of markers that identify important battle landmarks and explain the action that unfolded here, July 7, 1777. From that point, follow the path to find more markers as you walk the battlefield. Enjoy your walk. Hubbardton Battlefield is listed on the National Register of Historic Places and is managed by the State of Vermont Division of Historic Preservation.

(Hubbardton Marker)

visible on the hillside across the valley from Monument Hill.

As the British column reached Sucker Brook, the Americans were attacked. The Americans then retreated to positions atop Monument Hill, a good spot

---

Dawn Attack

Directly ahead, through the gap in the hill ran the military road which connected the American garrison at Mount Independence on Lake Champlain with sites on the Connecticut River. American forces used this road as their escape route from Fort Ticonderoga and Mount Independence. It was in this gap that the American pickets fired on British scouts about 5:00 a.m. on the morning of July 7, 1777. This marked the beginning of the battle. Down the valley below, the military road crossed Sucker Brook where sick and wounded soldiers had encamped the night before the battle. Colonel Nathan Hale had been left in charge of this group of invalids. The main part of his Second New Hampshire Regiment was encamped to the west of this group. Heavy fighting started about 7:00 a.m. Major Robert Grant and an advance British force attacked the Americans encamped near Sucker Brook where Grant was killed. Some of the Americans, who had gone down into the valley to assist the American soldiers encamped there, retreated back to the top where you are now standing.

(Hubbardton Marker)

Colonel Ebenezer Francis and his 11th Continental Regiment from Massachusetts encamped along this hilltop on the night of July 6, 1777. To the left, down the hill toward the Selleck Cabin was Seth Warner and his Green Mountain Boys. To the right was the rest of Colonel Nathan Hale's Second New Hampshire Regiment. On the morning of July 7th, British troops in hot pursuit of the American forces climbed these steep slopes to the crest of Monument Hill. Hampered by brush and fallen trees, the British in their bright red coats made excellent targets for the Americans positioned near a stone wall on the crest. As the British continued their assault up the hill, the Americans were eventually forced back across the field behind you.

(Hubbardton Marker)

British Flank near Mount Zion

Directly in front of you stands Majestic Mount Zion. From its summit, the whole battlefield can be seen and it may have served as a lookout for Tory and Indian scouts who were surveying the area for the British shortly before the battle. The valley below was less wooded in 1777 then it is now, probably cleared out by one of the nine families living in the area at the time. British Commander, General Simon Fraser sent some of his grenadiers and light infantry through these fields to flank the Americans and block the Castleton road to the south. Except for some minor skirmishing with the Green Mountain Boys, these British forces had an easy time overtaking the road during the battle.

(Hubbardton Marker)

for a defensive action. The British deployed and attacked the hill, but were immediately repulsed and even pursued in their retreat to their former position.

British Arrive, Americans Retreat

Most of the battle waged back and forth in this field until the Americans were finally forced across the Castleton Road to the east. They took up a position there behind a log and stone fence. After some heavy fighting, General Hale's Second New Hampshire Regiment crossed the road and flanked the British to the north. General Fraser, seeing his left flank under attack, sent word back to his rearguard for help. At a point when all seemed loss, some of Fraser's rearguard appeared. This small group, part of Baron Von Riedesel's larger gunswicker force, arrived just in time to disrupt Hale's flanking attempt. When Colonel Francis was killed, the Americans began moving away to the east. A running fight continued on top of the Pittsford ridge to your right until about 10:00 a.m. Colonel Hale and many of his weakened force later were found wandering in the woods and taken prisoner by the British. The battle was over with heavy losses on both sides. The British and Germans would claim victory because they held the field, but the American rearguard had done its job. The battle proved to be a stepping-stone to Bennington and Saratoga where the British General Burgoyne would surrender in October 1777.

(Hubbardton Marker)

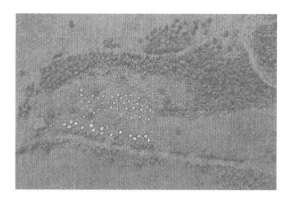

The Americans returned to the hilltop and again the British attacked and were repulsed. Thus the Battle continued for over an hour as the British attempted to flank the American defense. They, in turn, retreated to positions on the fence line east of the Military Road.

At this point the Brunswick troops under von Riedesel reached the scene and immediately attacked the American right with fixed bayonets, band blaring and drums drumming. American Colonel Francis received a mortal wound during the Brunswick attack. By this time, General St. Clair's troops had safely reached Castleton and the American troops could withdraw.

Although the American's were defeated, they had actually done precisely what was required in a rear guard action. They had fought the fully deployed enemy to a standstill and had given their main force time to move on. They had done so with skill and courage. Warner's men left the field with a great moral victory.

The Battle of Hubbardton involved about 2,000 troops and resulted in a total of about 600 casualties, or roughly 30 percent of all participating troops. The losses were approximately equal on both sides.

Col. Warner commanded.

Col. Francis was killed.

Col. Hale was captured.

The Green Mountain Boys fought bravely. The only battle fought in Vermont during the revolution on July 7, 1777.

(Hubbardton Marker)

The Hubbardton Battlefield Monument — The monument was erected in 1859. It is constructed from Vermont marble and surrounded by a cast iron fence. The monument marks the place where Colonel Ebenezer Francis is believed to be buried.

The leadership qualities and bravery under fire, shown by Colonels Warner and Francis during the conflict, had earned the highest respect of their adversaries. General von Riedesel, a veteran of many European campaigns, had especially admired these two youthful American officers. When Francis' body was found after the battle, Baron von Riedesel personally saw to it that this gallant young Colonel received a Christian burial, with full military honors rendered by a detachment from the Brunswick troops.

HUBBARDTON BATTLEFIELD TO MOUNT INDEPENDENCE

Mile Mark 123.8 — Escape the dive-bombing bugs that always seem to attack near the end of the walking trail at the Hubbardton Battlefield and continue north on Monument Road. Although this is not a marked highway, it eventually connects with VT Route 30.

Mile Mark 126.0 — Monument Road becomes a dirt road for a couple miles, but it's a hard packed dirt road, not even close to the conditions in 1777. The road does narrow a bit as you go through the mountain pass.

Mile Mark 126.6 — Watch for the turkey on the right. You'll have to look carefully; the turkey is well camouflaged.

Mile Mark 127.0 — Relax, the road returns to a welcome black tar once again.

Mile Mark 128.0 — Note the view off to the right of your car. On a clear day you can see down into the

valley. Lake Hortonia is off in the distance on the valley floor.

Mile Mark 129.4 — Monument Road ends at a stop sign. Turn right. This is Vermont Route 30 heading north.

Mile Mark 131.0 — Lake Hortonia is on the left as you drive along its eastern bank. It's a very picturesque lake with many lake homes on the western bank. Keep an eye out for slow moving milk trucks.

Mile Mark 132.7 — As you enter Sudbury, watch for views of Champlain Valley off in the distance as you come down the mountain.

Mile Mark 135.7 — A sign on the left provides directions to Mount Independence. Turn left onto

Mount Independence Military Road

Route to Hubbardton, 1777. After Ethan Allen seized Fort Ticonderoga in 1775, the Americans built a floating bridge from Fort Ticonderoga to Mount Independence completing the military road. Following Burgoyne's invasion, General St. Clair evacuated the forts, retreating down this road and across these hills to Hubbardton.

(Route 22A Marker)

Route 73 West, also the route to the Ticonderoga Ferry to New York.

Mile Mark 140.9 — Travel through the scenic town of Orwell, which is centered around the church, as many small New England towns are.

Mile Mark 141.1 — You will reach the intersection with Route 22A. Diagonally across the intersection is a military road marker. Travel across the intersection and continue following Vermont Route 73 West.

Mile Mark 141.4 — Watch for the sign to Mount Independence on the left. Bear left at this intersection. Once again, you are off the major highway and prepare for another dirt road in a few miles.

Mile Mark 142.9 — Pass a farmhouse on the right at the top of a hill. As you travel down the hill, note the views of Lake Champlain in the distance and Mount Defiance on the far side of the lake.

Military Road from Mount Independence to Hubbardton, 1777.

Placed by the Hands Cove Chapter of the Daughters of the American Revolution, 1933.

(Military Road Marker)

Mile Mark 143.2 — Watch for a stone, Military Road marker on the right at the bottom of the hill and the American Flags that surround the marker.

Mile Mark 144.4 — The road splits. Bear right to Mount Independence. The left fork leads down to Chipman's Point on the lake.

Mile Mark 144.9 — Note that you are now clearly on a penninsula with views of Lake Champlain on the right and East Creek on the left. The high ground to the front is Mount Independence with Mount Defiance behind.

Mile Mark 145.4 — Pass right through the middle of Audet's Lake Home Farm.

Mile Mark 145.8 — The road returns to dirt as you drive along the east bank of Lake Champlain. Watch for the split. Bear left up to Mount Independence

Mile Mark 146.3 — Arrive at the Mount Independence Visitor Center.

The center is an odd-looking building which could be mistaken for an arc that has run aground, but actually if you turn the whole building

**Mount Independence
Visitor Center**

9:30 AM - 5 PM

(Mount Independence Marker)

upside down, you'll have what was a major means of transportation on Lake Champlain during the Revolutionary War period: a bateau.

MOUNT INDEPENDENCE

Mount Independence is designated a National Historic Landmark. The site is covered by several miles of hiking trails that wind past the remains of batteries, blockhouses, hospital, barracks and other archaeological remnants of this once-bustling fort complex.

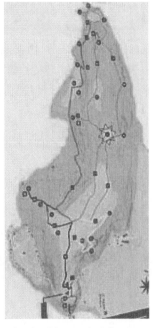

In the Visitor Center Museum, the story of military life atop the mount is told by larger-than-life military figures that are animated using audio and visual effects. Also, there are exhibits that present many of the artifacts recovered during recent archaeological investigations.

The Fort on Mount Independence — In the summer of 1776, atop this rugged hill along the shore of Lake Champlain, American troops began building this fort complex to guard against a British attack from Canada.

Mount Independence

In 1776, General Philip Schuyler identified this peninsula together with the old French fort across the narrows as the critical choke point for preventing the British from invading from the north. From July 1776 to July 1777, thousands of Americans garrisoned this site and Fort Ticonderoga. Just as construction of new artillery batteries was beginning here, news arrived that the continental congress declared independence. On July 28, 1776, Colonel Arthur St. Clair, the American brigade commander, read the Declaration of Independence to the assembled soldiers. After that day, East Point or Rattlesnake Hill, as this strategic height of land had been called, became known as Mount Independence. In July 1777, Burgoyne's British army forced the American troops to abandon this position. After the American evacuation, the British Army garrisoned the mount and continued work on the buildings and fortifications until November 1777 following the defeat of Burgoyne's army at Saratoga. The British rearguard burned all of the structures, abandoned the site and retreated to Canada.

(Mount Independence Marker)

The troops named it Mount Independence in honor of the Declaration of Independence.

Unlike Fort Ticonderoga across the lake, the fort mainly consisted of huts and houses. A large shore battery and a horseshoe-shaped battery were completed. A picket fort was under construction.

As expected, the British did lead a counterattack in 1776. But thanks to delays caused by a fleet of naval ships under the command of Benedict Arnold and the combined impressive sight of Mount Independence and Fort Ticonderoga, British General Guy Carleton retreated to Canada, abandoning an attempted invasion that year. The very next year, 1777, the opposite would occur.

Many American troops went home the winter of 1776-1777, reducing the force from 12,000 to just 2,500. Those remaining spent a horrible winter at Mount Independence. Many were sickly and a number froze to death.

In the spring of 1777, a few troops returned but not enough to properly garrison the forts. On July 5th, they evacuated the site when British General John Burgoyne's forces numbering about 8,000 began a penetration of the area. The evacuation was triggered by the

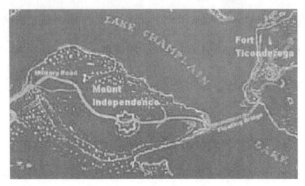

astonishing placement of cannon on Mount Defiance. Fort Ticonderoga and Mount Independence were supposedly easy targets from the top of Mount Defiance.

As the Americans retreated, the British pursued them down the old military road, but were halted at Hubbardton.

The Red Trail — Several trails at Mount Independence connect well-preserved remains of the Revolutionary War fortification. The trails pass through nearly four hundred acres of pasture and woodlands with vistas overlooking Lake Champlain and the surrounding countryside. Each of the trails are color-coded, but if you don't pay careful attention, you can easily get off on the wrong colored trail. For a short visit, the red trail, which is just a little over a half-mile, is recommended.

The Red Trail passes a line of remains that indicate the foundation site of a hospital. Begun in April 1777, the

hospital had a capacity of about 600. It was a two-floor, frame building of sawed planks, rather than blocks or logs. All of the hospital patients were evacuated during the American retreat on July 5 and 6, 1777, with the exception of four who were too sick to be moved.

The trail also passes a well-preserved, three-sided stone foundation, possibly an officer's quarters. Near the middle of the trail, there is a strategic lookout from a ledge that towers over Lake Champlain. The lookout is almost directly across from Mount Defiance. The LaChute River from Lake George and Fort Ticonderoga are clearly visible in the distance.

On the return from the lookout, you will pass a gravestone that is somewhat curious. The date on the stone is 1760, but historians believe it was placed in the 1800's.

MOUNT INDEPENDENCE TO FORT TICONDEROGA

Mile Mark 146.3 — Depart Mount Independence and return back to Vermont Route 73.

Mile Mark 150.7 — Cross over East Creek.

Mile Mark 151.0 — Reach the intersection with Vermont Route 73. Turn left and continue going west.

Mile Mark 154.0 — Norton's Gallery is on the left. Behind the gallery, you can see the area where the old military road once crossed Lake Champlain. Fort Ticonderoga is on the right; Mount Defiance is in the center on the far side of Lake Champlain. Mount Independence is on the left.

Mile Mark 155.2 — Reach the end of Route 73 and the intersection with Vermont Route 74. Turn left on Route 74 and go west.

Mile Mark 155.8 — Reach the Fort Ticonderoga Ferry, established in 1759. The ferry is actually a barge on cables that is driven back and forth across the lake. This is somewhat in keeping with the floating bridge that once crossed from Mount Independence to Fort Ticonderoga.

Note that as you cross the ferry (unless it's early spring or late fall), the fort is nowhere to be seen. The ferry trip confirms the main weakness of Fort Ticonderoga: its lack of a view to the north. Mount Defiance, however, can be clearly seen over the tree line.

Ahead of you, beyond the boat launch, a shore battery marked the first line of defense for revolutionary soldiers at Fort Ticonderoga in 1776. Three more redoubts reinforced the star-shaped fort on the ridge. Across Lake Champlain on the Vermont shore opposite Fort Ticonderoga, Mount Independence anchored the defense against British attack.

(Ticonderoga Ferry Marker)

> In late June 1777, General John Burgoyne prepared to lay siege to Fort Ticonderoga. He landed nearly 4,000 British regulars at Four Mile Point where the paper mill is now located. An additional 3,000 German mercenaries landed on the Vermont shore. Burgoyne expected to face the Gibraltar of the North, but brutal winter weather and a shortage of supplies had taken a terrible toll on the American troops defending these positions. When the British placed cannons atop Mount Defiance, American forces abandoned both Fort Ticonderoga and Mount Independence to the British and made a strategic retreat southward.
>
> (Ticonderoga Ferry Marker)

If you look to the south from the Ferry, you can see the area where the fort on Mount Independence was located. Even the ferry is not resistant to historical markers. You can find them on the ferry's side rail.

If you look to the north, on the eastern shore is the cove where the patriot forces consisting of:

- Benedict Arnold and his manservant,
- Edward Mott and about 16 volunteers from Connecticut,
- James Easton, John Brown and about 40 from the Berkshires, and
- Ethan Allen, Seth Warner and about 200 Green Mountain Boys,

made final preparations for taking Fort Ticonderoga. Their meeting headquarters, Hand's Cabin, can be seen on the banks of the cove, but is difficult to see from the ferry.

After driving off the ferry, continue following NY Route 74 going west.

Mile Mark 157.8 — Watch for the entrance gate to Fort Ticonderoga on the left. Go through the gate and enter the Carillon Battlefield. The Carillon Battlefield is where the French and the British battled for control of Fort  Ticonderoga during the French and Indian War. Most of the markers in the battlefield relate to this time-period.

Hut Sites

Within a radius of 1/2 mile were 150 huts occupied by American troops in the Revolution, 1776-1777.

(Carillon Battlefield Marker)

> Through this place passed General Henry Knox in the winter of 1775 -1776 to deliver to General George Washington at Cambridge the train of artillery from Fort Ticonderoga used to force the British army to evacuate Boston.
>
> Erected by the State of New York during the sesquentenial of the American Revolution.
>
> (Carillon Battlefield Marker)

However, there are two Revolutionary War markers. Watch for the Hut Marker on the right. Americans prepared to do battle with the British on the Carillon Battlefield in 1776 and 1777.

The other marker is a "Knox Trail" maker. In the winter of 1776-1777, Henry Knox led a transportation unit to carry artillery captured at Fort Ticonderoga to Boston in order to force the British from the city. The route he traveled is called the Knox Trail. Trail markers appear at many locations along US Route 4 on the way to Albany and along US Route 20 on the way to Boston.

> ### Garrison Cemetery
>
> Here are buried several hundred officers and men of the American Army, chiefly New York, New Jersey and Pennsylvania militia, 1775-1777.
>
> (Carillon Battlefield Marker)

> **R. I. P.**
>
> Here are interred the bones of 18 colonial soldiers found near the old military road in Ticonderoga village on November 1, 1924.
>
> (Carillon Battlefield Marker)

Continue up the entrance road. It opens up into a parking lot area with a field to the right and the entrance to the fort in the distance. The field contains a cemetery some distance away from the road. There are several markers and memorials in the cemetery.

Further back in the woods is a stone memorial that starts with a prayer -- "Rest in Peace".

Mile Mark 158.8 — Arrive at Fort Ticonderoga.

Ethan Allen's Route to Ticonderoga

10 May 1775 — When the men refused to proceed save under their own officers, Ethan Allen with Arnold at his side, and 83 Green Mountain Boys in support, storms and captures Fort Ticonderoga "in the name of the Great Jehovah and the Continental Congress."

(Fort Ticonderoga Exhibit)

FORT TICONDEROGA

When you arrive at Fort Ticonderoga, you step back in time. Fort Ticonderoga has been restored back to its original condition when the French first built the fort in 1755. To add to the realism, there are people dressed in period costume. There are also firing demonstrations and performances on the parade ground. There is always something going on to make a visit even more memorable.

In the fort's museum, you will find personal possessions of many of the major players, such as Ethan Allen and John Brown. For example, there is Ethan Allen's gun with his name engraved on the stock that he lent to Benedict Arnold.

Historic New York
Fort Ticonderoga

During the 18th century, when nations fought to control the strategic route between the St. Lawrence River in Canada and the Hudson River to the south, the fortification overlooking the outlet of Lake George into Lake Champlain was called "a key to a continent."

The French constructed here in 1755 the stronghold they named Carillon and made it a base to attack their English rivals. In 1758, Carillon, under Marquis de Montcalm, withstood assault by superior British forces. The next year, Jeffery Amherst's troops captured Carillon and forced the French to retreat from Lake Champlain. The British renamed the fortress Fort Ticonderoga.

During the American Revolution, Ethan Allen and the Green Mountain Boys captured Ticonderoga in a surprise attack, May 10, 1775. Cannon hauled from Ticonderoga to Boston helped George Washington drive the British from that city. In July 1777, General Burgoyne's invading army overwhelmed the American fort and Ticonderoga became British. Americans unsuccessfully attacked the fort in September 1777; later the British abandoned it.

In 1816, William Ferris Pell acquired the fort. His descendants began its restoration and in 1909 opened Ticonderoga to the public. Now the Fort Ticonderoga Association maintains the historic fort and its military museum.

(Fort Ticonderoga Marker)

YEAR	HELD BY	BESET BY	RESULT
1758	French	British	French
1759	French	British	British
1775	British	Americans	Americans
1776	Americans	British	Americans
1777	Americans	British	British
1777	British	Americans	British

There are also many maps, three-dimensional models, historical documents and revolutionary war art.

Near the visitor's entrance to Fort Ticonderoga, there is a welcoming marker. Missing from the marker is the

> Fort Ticonderoga (Carillon) successfully commanded the two waterways from the south but its position atop this ridge left the far side of the peninsula unprotected by cannon batteries. Army engineers in charge of the construction of the French Fort Carillon built an additional battery on the cliff at the end of the point to protect two landing sights, a shallow landing for bateau and cannons to the right and a cargo landing on the point to the north left where supply ships would tie up and unload. A covered way dug to the height of a man connected the fort to the battery.
>
> (Fort Ticonderoga Marker)

The Capture of Fort Ticonderoga
by Alonzo Chappel

incredible uniqueness of Fort Ticonderoga. No fort in the world has had such an active, yet short history. In two decades, Fort Ticonderoga was the center of attack by great nations as many as six times, four times during the American Revolution.

1775 Attack — In the early morning hours of May 10, 1775, Ethan Allen and Benedict Arnold advanced upon Fort Ticonderoga with only about half of their small army due to a shortage of crossing space. The boats that were supposed to be captured from Skenesborough had not arrived in time. The group approached the fort that was being held by a small British company of about twenty men under the command of Captain Delaplace.

They marched on the fort in column, three abreast. A sentry on guard at the entrance attempted to fire at the intruders, but his gun misfired (a common problem even today — firing

demonstrations held at the fort often misfire). The Americans stormed into the fort and Ethan Allen demanded surrender. When Captain Delaplace asked under whose authority, Allen responded, "the Great Jehovah and the Continental Congress." Delaplace surrendered and Ethan Allen and Benedict Arnold had taken the fort without firing a shot.

> "The sun seemed to rise that morning with a superior luster and Ticonderoga and its dependencies smiled on its conquerors who tossed about the flowing bowl and wished success to Congress and the liberty and freedom of America."
>
> — Ethan Allen, May 10, 1775.

The surrender of Fort Ticonderoga marked the first overt military action by Americans against the British in their quest for American independence. It was no doubt a daring and courageous act.

Later that year, General Henry Knox would begin moving cannon from Fort Ticonderoga to Boston. The same marker that appears on the Carillon Battlefield and at many other locations along the route that General Knox took also appears in the Place d'Arms at the center of the fort.

1776 Attack — In October of 1776, the British, led by Sir Guy Carleton, advanced against the Americans at Fort Ticonderoga. Under the command of General Horatio Gates and the support and leadership of Philip Schuyler, the

Americans were well dug-in and prepared for the British. After scouting the area and observing the impressive state of readiness at both Ticonderoga and Mount Independence, the British changed their minds. With a coming winter and not enough time to mount a major and timely offensive, the British retreated back to Canada. They would have arrived earlier, but they were delayed by Benedict Arnold's annoying American Navy on Lake Champlain. So, after just a few minor skirmishes, the two armies disengaged until next year.

John Burgoyne
by S. Hollyer

First 1777 Attack — In 1777, the British, led by General John Burgoyne, arrived plenty early enough on July 2nd and, this time, the American fortifications were not nearly as impressive. George Washington had turned his attention to Pennsylvania and did not expect the British to launch another major offensive against Fort Ticonderoga. It was the Americans who were not ready for a major offensive this time.

On July 4, 1777, British forces were observed moving cannons up the side of Mount Defiance, an action that

1776-1929

Through this entrance to the Place D'Arms
of the fort have passed

George Washington
Benjamin Franklin
Benedict Arnold
Horatio Gates
Anthony Wayne
Arthur St. Claire
Henry Knox
Philip Schuyler
Ethan Allen
Seth Warner
Richard Montgomery
Major Robert Rogers
Marquis de Montcalm
The Duc de Levis
Sir Jeffrey Amherst
Sir Guy Carleton
Major John Andre
Sir John Burgoyne
Thaddeus Kosciuszko

and a host of other great men
of our history.

Ye who tread in their footsteps,
remember their glory.

(Fort Ticonderoga Marker)

> ### Colonel John Brown of Pittsfield, Massachusetts
>
> Killed October 19, 1780 at Stone Arabia, New York on his 35th birthday. Was with Ethan Allen, May 10, 1775. Made a gallant attempt to retake the fort, September 17-22, 1777, but failed owing to the sturdy defense of Brigadier General Henry W. Powell. Colonel Brown destroyed the shipping and outer works, captured 225 British and Germans and released 100 American prisoners.
>
> This tablet was erected by the Massachusetts Society of the Colonial Dames of America, 1935.
>
> (Fort Ticonderoga Marker)

the Americans were not prepared for. From Mount Defiance, the defenses of both Fort Ticonderoga and Mount Independence were considered relatively easy targets. So, it was decided in a council of war on July 5th that General Arthur St. Clair would lead the Americans in retreat under the cover of darkness down the military road to Castleton. When the British discovered the American retreat, Burgoyne sent a detachment to pursue the Americans, but they were stopped at Hubbardton.

Second 1777 Attack — Burgoyne continued down Lake Champlain toward Albany leaving behind a detachment of about 200 men at Fort Ticonderoga. In September of 1777, Americans marched back to Fort Ticonderoga under the command of Colonel John

Brown.[1] Despite outnumbering the British five-to-one and essentially surrounding the fort and even targeting Fort Ticonderoga with cannon from the top of Mount Defiance, the British forces did not retreat or surrender. The Americans had no desire to storm the walls of Fort Ticonderoga. As a result, the British held Fort Ticonderoga and controlled Lake Champlain for the remainder of the war.

---

1. This is the same John Brown who helped plan the capture of Ticonderoga in 1775 in Pittsfield.

FORT TICONDEROGA TO FORT CROWN POINT

Mile Mark 158.8 — Depart Fort Ticonderoga. After passing back through the gate, turn left onto NY Route 74 going west.

Mile Mark 160.2 — Reach a stop sign at NY Route 22. Turn right and continue going west on Route 74.

This tablet marks the landing for the grand carry on the great war trail between the Indian tribes of the north and south country. It also marks the beginning of that carry between the lakes to avoid the falls and rapids which later became the military road built by the French in 1755.

The French saw mill, the first ever built in the Champlain Valley was erected in 1756 at the foot of the falls on the site of the present mills. In this saw mill, Abercromby, had his headquarters during his disastrous battle with Montcalm's forces at the French lines, July 8, 1758.

Washington and Franklin passed over this military road during the Revolution.

Presented to the Ticonderoga Society for the citizens of the town by the Ticonderoga Pulp Paper Company. Unveiled by the New York State Historical Association, October 4, 1910.

(Ticonderoga Marker)

If time permits, a visit to the town of Ticonderoga is recommended. Instead of turning right on Route 74, continue going straight into town. As you approach the village, look to your right and you will see a park and a waterfall. This drop is the last part of a 230-foot drop that the two-mile, LaChute River makes from Lake George to Lake Champlain. The French originally named Fort Ticonderoga, Fort Carillon due to the waterfalls on this river. They sounded like a carillon as the water gurgled its way to Lake Champlain. On the left is a "grand carry" marker.

Mount Defiance can be reached by heading into town on Montcalm Street, turning left at the first light, bearing left on Portage and turning left on Defiance Street. The top of the mountain is about a one-mile climb to the summit. The road is the same one cut by the British when they observed on July 2, 1777 that the American positions at Fort Ticonderoga and Mount Independence might be

115

vulnerable from the mountaintop.

There is a rotary at the end of Montcalm Street that will put you back on the road to Crown Point. In the middle of the rotary is a monument that recognizes Ticonderoga as a "Key to the Continent." Also on the rotary is the Ticonderoga Historical Society.

The road to Crown Point, Route 9N, is one quarter of the way around the rotary from Montcalm Street. Route 9N joins Route 22 at the next intersection.

About two and a half miles past the rotary is the small town called Streetroad. Many veterans of the Revolutionary War can be found buried in the town cemetary.

The military road marker on Route 22 is about two miles past the town of Streetroad.

Mile Mark 160.7 — Skipping the visit to Ticonderoga, you'll reach an intersection with Airport Road on Route 74. Turn right.

Mile Mark 162.9 — Pass the paper mill on the right. Try to imagine the thousands of British regulars that landed here prior to the advance on Fort Ticonderoga.

Streetroad Cemetery

Memorialized here are many first settlers, early doctors and supervisors, the town's first state senator, veterans of the Revolutionary War, War of 1812 and Civil War. Last burial of a Civil War veteran in 1936. Opposite were the Streetroad Commons, Church, School, Community Hall, Post Office and General Store.

(Streetroad Cemetery Marker)

Mile Mark 164.8 — Reach the intersection with Route 22. Watch for the military road marker just south of the intersection. Turn right, heading north.

**Old Military Road
Crown Point to Ticonderoga,
1689-1783**

Used by troops during the early colonial wars and during the American Revolution.

(Military Road Marker)

Mile Mark 168.8 — Reach the village of Crown Point. Turn right at the intersection just past the village and continue north on Route 22.

Mile Mark 172.4 — Reach the intersection with Route 17. Turn right going east. As you cross the train bridge just after the campground, look to your left and you will see Lake Champlain on the north side of the peninsula.

Mile Mark 176.5 — Reach the entrance to Fort Crown Point. Turn left before the bridge and drive to the Visitor Center.

FORT CROWN POINT

The Visitor Center includes exhibits that interpret the French, British, and American chapters of Crown Point's history. This historic site contains the impressive ruins of Fort Crown Point, including Fort St. Frederick (a fortress within a fort). The site was donated to the State of New York in 1910 and since that time, they have had to initiate several major stabilization efforts to keep the walls from falling down. Northeast winters cause the ground to expand and contract. This constant movement is a major problem for these old forts, including the restored Fort Ticonderoga to the south. You will likely observe collapsing walls supported by large timbers at both locations.

Following the French retreat from Crown Point in 1759, General Amherst embarked upon an ambitions plan to secure the area for Britain. An elaborate system of fortifications was begun on the point. At times, as many as 3,000 soldiers and artisans were engaged in the construction of Fort Crown Point, three smaller forts, called redoubts, several block houses, store houses, gardens and military roads. A village grew up close to the Fort wall with a tavern, store, apothecary shop, and the home of soldiers' families and retired officers. When control of Canada passed to Britain, at the end of the French and Indian War in 1763, construction ceased leaving one barracks building unfinished. In April 1773, a chimney fire spread from the soldier's barracks on the log walls of the fort resulting in the explosion of the powder magazine and the virtual destruction of the main fort. Troop strength at Crown Point was gradually reduced until only a tiny garrison remained to surrender the fort to American rebel troops commanded by Seth Warner in May of 1775.

(Crown Point Exhibit)

A century before the American Revolution, Crown Point was a vital and well-known area in the long struggle between France and Great Britain for the North American empire. Lake Champlain, a major highway for commerce and military supplies, was a target for control by both nations.

Fort Crown Point before the American Revolution – France, in 1734, began construction at Crown Point,

> British military engineer, John Montresor, recommended in May 1774 that Crown Point be the location of a new fortification made by enlarging and strengthening Grenadier Redoubt. Before British troops were sent from Montreal to implement Montresor's plan, the Revolutionary War began in Lexington and Concord.
>
> (Crown Point Exhibit)

the first substantial fortification in the Champlain Valley.

From 1734-1755, Fort St. Frederic at Crown Point gave France complete control of the Champlain Valley. Charles de Beauhamois, Governor of New France (Canada), actively encouraged settlement in the vicinity of Fort St. Frederic through generous royal grants of land, creating a French community around the fort. This combined military and civilian presence thwarted British expansion, and was an annoyance to British authorities. In 1759, the fort was taken by a combined force of British regulars and provincial troops numbering about 12,000 men.

The British immediately began construction of "His Majesty's Fort of Crown Point," as well as three redoubts and a series of blockhouses and redans, all interconnected by a network of roads. The fortification complex covered over three and one-half square miles, making it one of the most ambitious military engineering projects undertaken by the British in colonial North America.

Lake Champlain became a vital highway linking two diverse regions of British North America. Crown Point,

---

In May 1775, Seth Warner's American Forces captured the fort and Crown Point became a springboard for an invasion of Canada. General Richard Montgomery's force sailed down the lake in August 1775. Despite initial success in Montreal, the combined forces of Montgomery and Benedict Arnold were defeated at Quebec in December 1775. They retreated in disarray, riddled with smallpox, to Crown Point. Men died by the hundreds in makeshift field hospitals and were buried in mass graves.

(Visitor Center Exhibit)

located midway between Albany and Montreal, became the center of communication between New York and Canada.

Fort Crown Point during the American Revolution– At the outbreak of the American Revolution, the rebellious colonists looked to Crown Point to aid their cause.

The surrender of Fort Crown Point to American rebel troops commanded by Seth Warner in May of 1775 yielded 114 pieces of cannon and heavy ordnance sorely needed by the Americans. Colonel Henry Knox carried twenty-nine of these to Boston during that winter to force the British out of the city.

On May 23, 1775, Fort Crown Point was the meeting place for Ethan Allen, the Green Mountain Boys, Benedict Arnold and his small American Navy. Ethan Allen was returning from an attempted penetration of

---

While Arnold directed the construction of a Naval Squadron in the summer of 1776, Tripps fortified Crown Point in preparation of an expected British attack. Not until Arnold's squadron was badly beaten at the battle of Valcour Island in October did the last American troops abandon Crown Point to occupy Mount Independence overlooking Fort Ticonderoga.

(Visitor Center Exhibit)

> The last major action to involve Crown Point was Burgoyne's expedition in 1777. As support for his advancing army, a hospital was erected, a garrison of 200 men, was left at Crown Point that summer. Despite Burgoyne's defeat at Saratoga, the British retained absolute control of Lake Champlain with the garrison at Crown Point for the remainder of the war. Their ships cruised regularly between Crown Point and the naval shipyard at St. John. Crown Point did not return to American control until after the Peace Treaty, 1783.
>
> (Visitor Center Exhibit)

Canada, but was driven out by British troops. A month later, the British would take Allen prisoner in another unsuccessful attempt. Benedict Arnold and his navy would assume control of Crown Point and Lake Champlain. A month later, he would relinquish it to General Philip Schuyler's Northern Department of the Continental Army in a dispute over control.

In the fall of 1775, Schuyler and his army embarked from Crown Point with 1,700 troops for another attempt to conquer Canada. Beaten, they returned from Quebec in June 1776, to lie in makeshift hospitals at Crown Point.

In the fall of 1776, Lieutenant-Colonel Thomas Hartley and the 6th Pennsylvania Regiment heard the sounds of the naval engagement at Valcour Island from their entrenchments at Crown Point. The American Navy, once again led by Benedict Arnold, ambushed the British Naval Force, but was eventually forced to retreat down Lake Champlain. The regiment at Crown

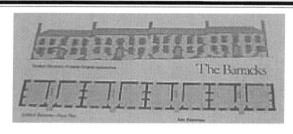

The Barracks

The barracks were constructed in fashionable Georgian style of the day uncommon in the northern interior of New York in the mid 18th century. The soldier's barracks is composed of four dwelling units of four rooms. Each doorway opens into a hallway flanked by two rooms. Originally the hallway contained a stairway to two rooms on the second floor. Between 12 and 18 soldiers occupied each room. Officers were allowed one or more rooms according to rank. Non-commissioned officers were quartered two to a room. Soldiers were allotted 1/2 cord of wood per room each week for cooking and heating and one pound of candles for light. Six beds and twelve blankets were provided for a room housing 12 men as were an iron pot, candlestick, bucket and ax. Clean sheets, when available, were issued once a month during the 1760's.

(Crown Point Marker)

Point also retreated southward to Fort Ticonderoga and Mount Independence.

Crown Point was a staging area for the British in both 1776 and 1777. After the Americans abandoned Crown Point, the British assembled their troops here. Delayed by the American Navy, Sir Guy Carleton arrived here with his troops in October of 1776, but retreated north for the winter shortly thereafter. British General John Burgoyne's army arrived here in June of 1777. Crown Point remained under British control until the end of the war.

FORT CROWN POINT TO THE MARITIME MUSEUM

Mile Mark 177.1 — Leave Fort Crown Point going east on Route 17.

Mile Mark 177.7 — Cross the Champlain Bridge and return to Vermont. Pass Chimney Point on the right.

> ### Chimney Point
>
> This strategic point on Lake Champlain was occupied by Native Americans for thousands of years. In 1690 Jacobus deWarm built a small stone fort here. The French built a wooden stockade in 1731, erecting Fort St. Frederic across the lake in 1734. After the 1759 French retreat to Canada, the houses were burned, leaving only the chimneys and the name — Chimney Point.
>
> The British built a military road in 1759 to connect Fort No. 4 (Charlestown, NH) to their new fort at Crown Point, NY: the road ended two miles to the south. They also built earthworks at Chimney Point, as did American Revolutionary forces in 1776.
>
> The tavern, built in the 1780s, was visited in 1791 by Thomas Jefferson and James Madison. In the early 1900s, it was a summer resort.
>
> Vermont Division for Historic Preservation—2002
>
> (Chimney Point Marker)

The museum at Chimney Point explores Vermont's ethnic heritage.

Mile Mark 178.3 — Bear left at a fork in the road and head toward Vergennes. The right fork goes to Middlebury. All of these places lie in an area that was left as a *demilitarized zone* after the loss of Fort Ticonderoga and Crown Point. Many of those that stayed in the area were British sympathizers or determined-to-stay Vermonters, some were too weak or too poor to leave, and many were farmers who periodically came to plant, tend, and harvest their crops. All who stayed in the area did so at their own risk. The British did send patrols from Canada and so did the Vermont Militia from the Rutland area.

Watch for the military road marker on the island in the middle of this intersection.

Mile Mark 179.8 — Pass the John Strong House on the left — the local home of the Daughters of the American Revolution.

Near this spot on the shore of the lake was the northern terminal of the Crown Point Military Road built by Gen. Amherst in 1759.

Erected by the Rhoda Farrano Chapter D.A.R.
1929

(Chimney Point Marker)

Mile Mark 180.3 — Reach the Adison Country Store. Turn left onto Lake Street.

Mile Mark 186.1 — Watch for the directional sign for the Maritime Museum. Bear right.

Mile Mark 187.4 — Enter the town of Panton. Turn left at the intersection, watch for another directional sign and bear left.

Mile Mark 189.9 — Pass Button Bay State Park on the left.

Mile Mark 190.6 — Reach the intersection with Basin Harbor Road. Bear left and watch for the entrance to the Maritime Museum on the right. Enter the parking lot.

Mile Mark 191.1 — Arrive at the Lake Champlain Maritime Museum. The museum is open daily from 10 AM to 5 PM, May – mid October. If you arrive too late on your **Revolutionary Day**, it is well worth returning to.

LAKE CHAMPLAIN MARITIME MUSEUM

The Lake Champlain Maritime Museum is dedicated to preserving the maritime history and heritage of the Champlain Valley. The site includes boat building, artifact conservation, exhibits, videos and replica vessels manned by sailors in period clothing. Many of the exhibits cover the Revolutionary War Period.

The highlight of any visit to the museum is a tour of the full-sized, 54-foot replica of Benedict Arnold's 1776 gunboat, the Philadelphia II. The vessel is rigged, armed and afloat in the museum's North Harbor. Occasionally, they present firing demonstrations using the cannons on board.

Behind the boat shed, they have a working model of an 18th century blacksmith

shop. In the shop, you can watch live demonstrations, including the forging of iron fittings for ships such as the Philadelphia II.

In the Revolutionary War building, they have a "Key to Liberty" exhibit. In the building, the complete story of Benedict Arnold's 1776 naval fleet on Lake Champlain is told. It includes ship models, interactive learning stations, historical maps, pictures and videos. One video shows the underwater exploration of a surviving gunboat

discovered in 1997 at the bottom of Lake Champlain. The vessel still lies on the bottom of the lake and its exact location remains a secret.

The "Key to Liberty" exhibit is one of the largest exhibits in the country dedicated in, great part, to Benedict Arnold's 1776 naval fleet. Naval museums at the US Naval War College in Newport, RI and the US Naval Academy in Annapolis, MD hardly mention this part of US naval history. No doubt, if Benedict Arnold had not sold-out to the British at West Point and then spilled American blood by leading British troops near the end of the war, he would be the Navy's first hero instead of today's John Paul Jones.

What's fortunate about the existence of the Lake Champlain Maritime Museum is that the heroism displayed by Benedict Arnold's sailors in 1776 will not be forgotten.

MARITIME MUSEUM TO SHELBURNE

Mile Mark 191.1 — Depart the museum.

Mile Mark 191.5 — Continue going straight on Basin Harbor Road.

Mile Mark 193.5 — Travel along Otter Creek on the left. This is the same creek that was crossed at Meads Falls in Rutland. Otter Creek also goes through Middlebury and Vergennes.

Mile Mark 195.8 — Reach an intersection with Panton Road in Vergennes. Turn left onto the road.

Mile Mark 197.0 — Pass the Goodrich plant on the left.

Mile Mark 197.2 — Reach the intersection with West Main Street. Turn left onto West Main Street and cross Otter Creek.

On October 24, 1778, Major Christopher Carleton led a battalion-sized force south on Lake Champlain from Canada. The force consisted of British regular forces, American loyalists, German mercenaries and Indians totaling approximately 450 men. The purpose of "Carlton's Raid" was to take prisoners and supplies and destroy buildings or material that could be used to support invasions into Canada. They landed on the east side of Lake Champlain near Crown Point. On November 6th, they moved inland to Otter Creek at Middlebury. They found Middlebury abandoned, but before heading down river toward Vergennes, they torched most of the town. Carleton reached Vergennes on November 8th, found a few inhabitants, and took them prisoner. Carleton also struck other areas west and south of Vergennes. When he returned to Canada on November 12th, he had 39 prisoners and reported the destruction of "4 months provisions for 12,000 men."

Mile Mark 198.1 — Go through the picturesque town of Vergennes and reach the intersection with US Route 7 just east of the town. Turn left and rejoin US Route 7 going north.

Mile Mark 208.4 — As you come down the hill into Shelburne, VT, note the panoramic view with the Adirondack mountains on the left, Lake Champlain in the foreground and the Green Mountains on the right.

Mile Mark 210.6 — Pass the Vermont Teddy Bear Company on the right.

Mile Mark 211.2 — Watch for the Shelburne Museum on the left. If you arrive too late to visit the museum on your **Revolutionary Day**, it is also well worth returning to.

Arrive in Shelburne.

SHELBURNE, VERMONT

Shelburne Museum — The museum is a collection of architectures, artifacts and art from America's past. Many items in the collection date back to the Revolutionary War period.

One of the oldest homes is the Preston House. It was built in 1773 in Hadley, Massachusetts and moved to its present site in 1955.

Another old home is the Dutton House. It was built in Cavendish, Vermont in 1782. Both houses are of the old "saltbox" style that was commonly found in colonial New England.

The museum's Stagecoach Inn was once on the old colonial route paralleling today's US Route 7 in Charlotte[1] in 1783. Charlotte is just south of Shelburne near Lake Champlain.

Although the Revolutionary War did not officially end until November of 1783, hostilities began to subside after America's victory at Yorktown in October 1781. With the construction of inns like the Stagecoach Inn, life in northern Vermont was returning back to normal.

One of the museum's most popular exhibits is the steamship Ticonderoga, America's last vertical beam, side-wheel, passenger steamboat from 1906. The ship is grounded at the museum and in pristine condition.

Village Center — Just north of the museum is the village center. Today, the village is a peaceful, picturesque Vermont town.

During the Revolutionary War, Shelburne was inhabited, but not so peaceful. On March 12, 1778, the village was attacked by a small British force led by a Tory named Philo. Philo was a Shelburne resident and led this attack against his own neighbors. The force included Tories and Indians. Fortunately for the neighbors, they had noticed that the British sympathizers were leaving the area, which tipped-off the impending attack and gave them time to prepare. They fortified the home of Moses Pierson and obtained support from the Vermont Militia stationed in Clarendon.[2] The attack on Shelburne was repulsed and the British force retreated back to Canada.

---

1. Pronounced Sha-Lot by Vermonters.
2. Clarendon is south of Rutland just off US Route 7.

SHELBURNE TO BURLINGTON

Mile Mark 211.4 — Depart the town of Shelburne.

As you continue north on US Route 7, you will likely encounter heavy traffic as you go through South Burlington and a series of lights that brings to mind the slow going into Rutland[1].

Mile Mark 213.9 — As you creep up US Route 7, watch on the right for what is not the Ethan Allen Homestead. However, this is an example of the home that most people think of when you mention Ethan Allen. Furniture has, unfortunately for history, made Ethan Allen better known than the historical person for whom it was named. One wishes the company would add a little historical corner to their ads in recognition of their real roots.

Mile Mark 216.0 — Reach the intersection with Interstate 189. Continue straight on US Route 7 North.

Mile Mark 218.1 — Pass the intersection with Main Street and turn left onto Pearl Street near the University of Vermont. Follow Pearl Street through downtown Burlington. Continue through the downtown area to the end of Pearl Street and down to Battery Park.

From Battery Park, there is a beautiful view of Lake Champlain. Across the lake on the New York side and to the north is Valcour Island, the site of the 1776 naval engagement between the American Navy under

Benedict Arnold and the British Navy under Sir Guy Carlton.

After the Revolutionary War, the naval engagements with the British would return to the lake during the War of 1812. Battery park was a witness to the Battle of Lake Champlain as noted by a marker in the park.

From Battery Park, turn right onto Vermont 127 North.

Mile Mark 221.2 — Bear right off of Vermont 127 at the Ethan Allen Homestead sign. Take the next right also marked with a homestead sign.

Mile Mark 221.5 — Arrive at the Ethan Allen Homestead in Burlington.

---

1. As a young engineer in the early 70's, this stop-and-go exercise on US Route 7 was part of the author's daily, dreaded commute from his home in Shelburne to Burlington's General Electric plant where he worked. Recent efforts have done little to alleviate the problem.

Winooski Valley Park District
Ethan Allen Homestead Historic Site
Home of Ethan Allen
(Homestead Marker)

ETHAN ALLEN HOMESTEAD
BURLINGTON, VERMONT

The Ethan Allen Homestead is preserved as a part of a wetlands park along the Winooski River. The park is a municipal partnership that preserves the beauty of the river valley. Near the entrance is a wooden walking bridge that spans Vermont 127. If you pass under this unique looking bridge, you missed the entrance.

As you enter the park, there is a small parking area on the right in front a large bog that is part of the wetlands park. Depending upon the time of the year, you can see the homestead in the distance overlooking the bog. The home sits up

on a hill on a small strip of land between the Winooski River and the bog.

Further down the road is a large parking lot in front of the Education Center.

Ethan Allen Homestead — The Education Center provides guided tours of the homestead from early May

> ## The House
>
> Allen's 24-foot wide, one-and-one-half story, post-and-beam, clapboard-sheathed home was built to his specifications from wood sawn at his brother Ira's mill. It was a little more elaborate than a frontier settler's home of the period, but less grand than Ira's house at the Winooski Falls. The massive stone and brick center chimney, and the upstairs rooms under the eaves are typical.
>
>
>
> (Education Center Exhibit)

through mid October. The tour includes a walk through the homestead and the historic gardens. It begins in the education center with a multi-media show. The center also includes a museum and gift store.

The center is closed in the evenings but the park that surrounds the homestead is open until dusk.

Riverside Walk — There is a short walk that begins on the left side of the Education Center. The pathway leads between the homestead and the Winooski River down to the river and through the bog.

There is no doubt that Ethan and his wife, Fannie,

The Land

Late in 1787, Ethan Allen arrived here with wife Fanny, five children and three servants. He had traded with his brother, Ira, for the acreage, and contracted with him for building materials. Near the house the Allens probably had a vegetable garden, dooryard and orchard, and Fanny may have had flowers. Outbuildings likely included a barn, woodshed and privy.

"I have lately arrived at my new farm of 14 hundred acres in which there are three hundred and fifty acres of choice river intervale, rich upland meadow interspersed with the finest of wheat land and pasture land well watered and is by nature equal to any tract of the same number of acres that I ever saw. I have about forty acres under improvement."

-- Ethan Allen, November 1787

(Education Center Exhibit)

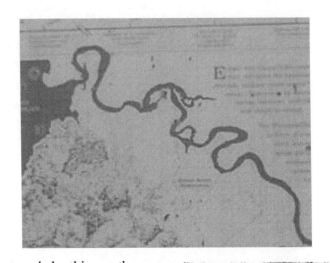

traveled this path many times as the river was a major means of transportation, even in winter. Ethan Allen purportedly died of a heart attack bringing supplies by sleigh from a frozen Lake Champlain and up the Winooski River. Unfortunately, his death occurred just a few short years after moving in to the house.

At the bottom of the hill, there is a wetlands marker at the river. There is also a series of markers along "Wetland Walk North." This walking trail can be reached by following the bike path away from the river for a short distance. At the end of the trail is a set of stairs that takes you by the other side of the homestead.

Wetland Walk North

Ethan and Fannie Allen moored their boat near here when they occupied the homestead. Both Ethan Allen and the Abernacki Indians relied on the Winooski River as a transportation route.

Travel was by canoe and other watercraft in the spring, summer and fall and on foot or by horse and sleigh in winter.

The Winooski River helped shape the landscape in front of you. As the river moved back and forth across the land it formed broad fertile plain. Low lying areas became wetlands. The fertile plains and waters attracted Native Americans and Europeans looking for fish, wild game and farmland.

(Homestead Marker)

What are Wetlands?

Wetlands are wet areas that at least sometimes have water-logged soils or are covered with a shallow layer of water. Wetlands may be marshes, swamps, swamp-forests or bogs. You can find all of these kinds of wetlands in Vermont.

As you follow the walkway notice the changes in vegetation as the soils become progressively more wet. This wetland, part of the Burlington-Colchester Intervale, is the site of an old channel of the Winooski River. The terrace above you, the site of the Ethan Allen Homestead, forms the natural boundary of the wetland.

Wetlands, in spite of their former reputation as wasteland, are now valued in many ways. They support a wide variety of wildlife and plants, help control floods and filter surface water. People have historically used this wetland for pasture and as a source of wild game and useful plants.

(Homestead Marker)

Overnight in Essex — A recommended nearby spot for the evening is the Inn at Essex. The inn is a AAA, four-star country hotel in Essex, Vermont. The rooms are furnished with period reproduction furniture, many with fireplaces. The restaurants at the inn are staffed by faculty and students of the New England Culinary Institute. Dining is always a remarkable event. Reservations are a must (802-878-1100).

To reach the inn, go back to Route 127 and follow it north about 3 miles past Malletts Bay and to its end at the intersection with US Route 7. Continue across the intersection and follow Severance Road until it ends at an intersection near Route 289. Bear left and follow the signs to Route 289. Take Route 289 to Exit 10. The inn is next to Exit 10.

"But, as in the present Instance, when Laws, in their original Design and Administration, are degenerated from the good Ends for which the Laws and Government were instituted, terminating in the Ruin and Destruction of the Society it should secure and protect; from the same Principles, viz.: self-preservation, the Subjects are obliged to resist, and depose such Government.

-- Ethan Allen, 1774

BIBLIOGRAPHY

Allen, Ethan, **The Narrative of Colonel Ethan Allen,** Applewood Books, Bedford, Massachusetts, 1779.

Bobrick, Benson, **Angel in the Whirlwind,** Penguin Books, New York, 1997.

Cheney, Cora, **Vermont, The State with the Story Book Past**[1], New England Press, Shelburne, Vermont, 1999.

Hamilton, Edward P., **Fort Ticonderoga, Key to a Continent,** Little, Brown and Company, Boston, 1964.

Lake Champlain Maritime Museum, "Map and Guide", 2001.

New York Office of Parks, "Bennington Battlefield, State Historic Site", 1997.

Office of Parks, Recreation and Historic Preservation, Department of Environmental Conservation, State of New York, "Crown Point, State Historic Site", 1998.

Purcell, L. Edward and David F. Burg, Editors, **The World Almanac of the American Revolution**, Pharos Books, New York, 1992.

Secker-Walker, Jocelyn, **Ethan Allen, Highlights in the Life of Vermont's Folk Hero**, Ethan Allen Homestead Trust, Burlington, Vermont, 1993.

Vermont Division for Historic Preservation, "Hubbardton Battlefield State Historic Site", 1996.

Vermont Division for Historic Preservation, "Mount Independence, State Historic Site", 1997.

Washington, Ida H. and Paul H. Washington, **Carleton's Raid**, Cherry Tree Books, Weybridge, Vermont, 1977.

---

1. Cora Cheney's book is written for young readers, but young and old alike will enjoy this book.

Raymond C. Houghton is a freelance historian and sole proprietor of Cyber Haus of Delmar, NY. He is a retired college professor, former government bureaucrat, Vietnam Veteran and one-time, General Electric employee. He has honors from the Department of Commerce, is listed in Who's Who in America and holds a doctorate from Duke University.